The Art of Friendship

The Art of Friendship

Christine Leefeldt

Ernest Callenbach

Pantheon Books
New York

Library of Congress Cataloging in Publication Data

Leefeldt, Christine, 1941-
    The art of friendship.
    1. Friendship. I. Callenbach, Ernest, joint author.
II. Title.
BJ1533.F8L44   158'.2   79-1893
    ISBN 0-394-50460-7

Design by Irva Mandelbaum

Manufactured in the United States of America

First Edition

To our friends

Contents

Acknowledgments

Because we promised anonymity to the hundreds of people we interviewed for this book, we cannot properly acknowledge the immense help we received from them. (To preserve their privacy, we have changed names, occupations, and other identifiable details.) Without them and the friendly aid they extended to us, sometimes through happy reminiscences but sometimes through painful self-searching, we would literally not have been able to write this book. We hope that the book is a fitting return for their generosity.

—Christine Leefeldt and
Ernest Callenbach

Berkeley, California
Spring 1979

The Art of Friendship

1.
Rediscovering Friendship

When family ties falter, when love affairs or marriages end, friends relieve our loneliness, fulfill our need for affection, and bolster our morale. Making and keeping friends may be among the most important things you can do for yourself; and relating sensitively and meaningfully to friends is an art you can learn.

Though little has been written about it, friendship is a major, indeed crucial, factor in emotional health and happiness. The personal stories in this book, like some recent statistical research by behavioral scientists, indicate that friendship contributes significantly to our growth and survival. Yet, though we may occasionally wonder if our friendships are as deep and rewarding as they might be, we seldom reflect on them in any focused or systematic way.

The people from across the country with whom we talked while researching this book were intrigued and excited by the opportunity to discuss their friendships. The many stories they generously shared with us often illuminated the subtle processes of friendship—how it begins, deepens, changes, and sometimes ends. We explored with them how they overcame difficulties in relating and how they resolved problems with their friends.

The people we spoke with include married people in conventional families and single and divorced persons, of various ages, occupations, and sexual preferences. Despite their diverse backgrounds and lifestyles, these people clearly indicated that friendship is a challenging, rewarding, and supportive force in their lives.

Each friendship has its own special quality. Some friendships are based on shared optimism, the two friends cheerfully encouraging each other but preferring not to share their bleaker moments. Other friends doggedly sustain each other, year after year, through the vicissitudes of life, commiserating over every pain, every heartbreak. Some friendships are private; if the friends find themselves in the company of others, they suddenly feel constrained with each other, and the vitality of their interaction diminishes. On the other hand, there are friendships that seem able to exist only when the people involved are in the midst of a large, active social circle; if the friends find themselves alone, their interaction becomes flat and uninteresting. As we researched this book, we were fascinated to observe and reflect on the intricate dance of emotion and commitment from which each friendship draws its character and strength.

Friendship abounds in paradoxes and contrasts. While it is difficult, perhaps impossible, for people of markedly unequal status to be true friends, friendship is never altogether equal or reciprocal: Jeffrey may consider David to be his best friend, but David regards Mel as *his* best friend. Some people feel that the friend's declaration "I like you" is a "purer" statement than "I love you." In love relationships, they believe, people often feel too vulnerable to be altogether frank with each other, whereas in friendships they feel less pressured, more objective. Some people think of friends as people with whom they'll spend time when their lovers aren't available; others say that friendship is more demanding than a love relationship, and they think it's easier to find a lover than a friend. Some believe sex and friendship must be kept scrupulously separate, while others find it comfortable for the two to coexist. Some friendships thrive in a context of shared interests; others have outlived them and seem to survive only because the past itself has become a shared interest.

The fact is that there is something irreducibly mysterious about the genesis of friendships. People may be in touch with each other over a long period of time, with no friendship developing between them. On the other hand, two people may just "click" and an instant rapport is established, even though they have known each other only briefly. There is also a kind of transferability of friendship: when you meet the friend of a friend, you are somehow predisposed toward friendship with that person, too. Sharing an "enemy"—a boss, a rival—can be as stimulating for friendship as sharing a friend. Sometimes, one person indicates to another, either verbally or nonverbally, a need for assistance and the willingness to receive it, whereupon the other person somehow acknowledges the need and signifies a willingness to help—not out of pity but out of kindred feeling. Such mutual "exposure" opens people up to each other and encourages further interactions on an emotionally intimate level.

It has been difficult for Americans to think seriously about friendship because we have no precise terminology to distinguish among long-term or lifelong friends, close friends, family or couple friends, casual friends, work friends, and acquaintances. (There are even occasions when we extend the term "friend" to include people we barely know.) Moreover, no one yet seems to have offered an entirely satisfactory definition of friendship, and probably no one ever will, because friendship is such a complex and ever-changing phenomenon. For our purposes here, however, a friend is simply someone you spend time with because it's enjoyable to do so and not because it's profitable, useful, or necessary. Friendship is a free and equal nonutilitarian relationship.

Of course, friends do many things for each other, and we will explore these exchanges at length. But the benefits we reap from our friendships are neither the cause of nor the basis for friendship so much as the consequences of it. Indeed we tend to love people we help more readily than we love people who help us. The friendship bond thrives upon a sense of generosity and mutuality, not sharp dealing and rational calculation of gains and losses. Such sharing behavior, we suspect, goes back very far in our biological evolution and is probably far more "human" than the cost-benefit analysis we so often allow to displace or outweigh emotional ties. Through friendships freely offered, we can sustain each other emotionally without encroaching on each other—a precious and touching human capacity, and doubly valuable in a society which operates as if everything has a price. Americans too seldom praise each other for being good at friendship, although we give ample recognition to ambition, power, and physical attractiveness. Perhaps this is a result of our apparent difficulty in pinpointing the qualities which make our friendships successful—though we often place a very high value on the happiness friendship brings.

Each friendship exists in a complex social network that creates both opportunities for friendship to thrive and obstacles to its development. We were endlessly fascinated by the strategies people adopt to maintain friendships despite the stresses of family responsibilities, marriage, love affairs, and power relationships.

Many people are conscious of obstacles that impede friendships in our society. Early family influences may inhibit us: "Friends come and go; it's family that counts," proclaimed the father of one person we talked to. We all face difficulties in making time for friends, solving conflicts with marital commitments, and overcoming barriers raised by age differences, class, power, lifestyle, and sex roles. But among people who successfully surmount these difficulties we found an adventurousness, a willingness to be open to contacts with new people, a creativity that allowed them to somehow break through barriers that too many people let separate them.

Those who maintain a flexible and resourceful attitude in other areas of their lives are especially good at coping ingeniously with the fluctuations of energy, time, and distance which any important friendship undergoes. They recognize that a friendship is worth fighting to preserve: they take thought about their friendships, bring conflicts and problems out into the open for mutual discussion, and persevere in resolving them. But they recognize that sometimes, despite their best efforts, friendships do founder in irreconcilable disagreements, life changes, or the overwhelming impact of external events.

Pursuing friendship adventurously is growing easier and more rewarding as a result of recent welcome changes in American society. People are struggling, in both the personal and the professional spheres, to overcome the stereotypes about what it means to be "married," "single," "divorced," "old," "young," "black," "white," "female," "male," "gay," and "bisexual." If we seize the opportunity, these redefinitions of ourselves can allow us to explore new frontiers in friendship.

Whether or not we have ever consciously analyzed the processes of friendship, we know we feel comfortable and alive when we are with friends. We're interested and responsive, physically relaxed and trusting; we're intrigued by our differences and reassured by our similarities. Friends, like jazz musicians, "play" together variations on the themes of their relationship, and their basic empathy enables them to weather even difficult, disharmonious times.

There are no "typical" friendships in this book but rather a varied array of friendships that arise from many different situations and exemplify different patterns of affection and sharing, need and response. While there are distinct recurrent features in most friendships, these are not bound by the kind of traditional contracts and obligations that govern our parental or marital relationships. They are as different as the people involved in them. But there are nonetheless certain essentials of friendship—equality, loyalty, trust, candor, mutual respect—and they are ineluctable.

We wrote this book because we realized that friendship, though it is one of the major forces holding us together in social networks, enabling us to live as more than a welter of atomized individuals and couples, has been virtually ignored in recent psychological writings. Innumerable books have been published about marital problems, sex problems, problems in escaping the emotional scripts we learned as children. We have been exhorted to clarify our couple relationships, open our marriages, be creative in our divorces, be our own best friends. Lay persons and psychotherapists alike have too often ignored friendships and the resources they provide, narrowly assuming that all that is important in human life happens either within the individual or within the couple relationship.

We knew this was not enough. Both of us have had our share of chaos and catastrophe; and through painful experience, we've learned the vital importance of long-lasting friendships to our own emotional stability, well-being, and happiness. We hope that our book will enable others to share our sense of wonder and gratitude at the marvelous human achievement which is friendship.

2.

Friends and Families

We usually think of our friends and families as totally separate elements of our adult lives—indeed, often opposed elements. Yet, the mysterious aspects of personality which will later enable us to make and keep friends develop from our early experiences with our parents, who also provide the models of behavior that expose us to the broad spectrum of relating possibilities, from generosity to selfishness, love to indifference, perceptiveness to insensitivity, openness to suspicion—the polarities that define whether our later friendships will thrive or wither.

Clues to greater enjoyment of the present may often be found by scrutinizing the past, but we rarely apply this principle to our friendships. A few adolescents may question and criticize the kinds of friends and friendships their parents have, but for most of us this stage comes later—if at all—when we are forced by feelings of loneliness or friendlessness to evaluate how we deal with friendships and to try to understand the strengths and limitations of the models of friendship provided by our families. Tracing your friendship history back to its family roots may give you insight into aspects of your upbringing which, years later, may still be damaging or restricting your friendships. It may also enable you to identify positive, growth-promoting elements of your family friendship

legacy which you can build upon in your current relationships.

The origins of our friendship history go back to such an
early age that we literally cannot remember them. We
first develop rudimentary friendships around age 2, and
some of the most intriguing are with imaginary friends.
Though Natalie has no direct memory of this period, her
mother and father have often told her stories about her
imaginary friend, Chakka. When her parents first heard
Natalie talking about Chakka, they assumed Chakka was
a playmate from Natalie's child-care center, but they soon
found there was no child there with such a name. They
also overheard Natalie having long though fragmented
conversations when she was alone, and when they asked
what she was doing, she would reply that she was talking
with Chakka. She also "read" books to Chakka, and they
played complicated games together.

Though Natalie always seemed happy when Chakka
was around and spent long periods of time contentedly
playing with her, Natalie's parents were somewhat concerned that Natalie's attachment to this imaginary friend
might be preventing her from being as sociable with real
children as they wanted her to be. Their pediatrician,
however, reassured them that imaginary playmates are
common among firstborn or only children, such as Natalie; she also pointed out that the creation of imaginary
friends is often a manifestation of intelligence and initiative. She reminded them that Natalie had progressed
quite normally through the usual stages in her relationships to the world and other persons: as an infant, she had
had little sense of the boundary between herself and her
father and mother; in babyhood, she gradually perceived
that she was a separate being and that her parents,
though still connected to her by intense and reliable
bonds, were somehow split-off, independent people. The

pediatrician further explained that Natalie's future capacity to relate to others as independent yet trustworthy kindred spirits would grow out of this early combination of feelings about her parents as people separate from yet somehow extensions of herself.

Her parents had noticed that, with Chakka, Natalie began a more complex, reciprocal type of interaction than she had experienced in her side-by-side play with other children, practicing a variety of roles she could not yet manage with them. She spoke to Chakka and then invented Chakka's responses. Chakka was, of course, a projection of aspects of Natalie's own personality. If Chakka was "bad," Natalie could imitate her parents and chastise Chakka; if Natalie was bored or unhappy, she could have Chakka tell her stories or think up some mischief.

Clearly, Chakka was Natalie's first friend. In her later nursery-school years, Natalie, like many children who have imaginary friends, proved to be a self-starter, good at inventing play activities and more adept than other children at talking with and relating to adults. Chakka had given her practice in friendship skills from an early age and perhaps had helped her unconsciously resolve conflicts with her parents. By age 3 or 4, Natalie had learned interactive, equal play with children and had developed a consciousness of give and take, an ability to share and take turns, some capacity to resist bullying, and a sense of how other children were likely to react to her. As she focused attention on her real playmates, some of whom became friends, Chakka gradually disappeared from Natalie's life.

Natalie feels fortunate that her parents took pains to understand her imaginary friendship and accepted the role Chakka played in her early life. She believes that her parents' attitude continued through her later years—they were also accepting of her childhood and adolescent friends—and she feels this has helped her to develop and maintain the close, easygoing friendships she enjoys today.

In their kindergarten and early school years, children gradually explore their capacities for interaction with others. They gain a sense of their own power to influence relationships; they test themselves against the pressures exerted by their peers; and they begin to learn standards for behavior. During this period, children make definite choices in companions and realize that others make such choices as well; they begin to know what it means to say, "You are my friend." Parents generally find this period easy to handle. Their attitudes toward their children's friendships are often tested, however, in the period after age 8 or 9, when children adopt "best friends."

By this age, children have begun to spend considerable amounts of time on their own, after school and on weekends, away from the family. They sometimes develop passionate identifications with older schoolmates whom they idolize; and they attach themselves to best friends, to whom they are intensely devoted, with whom they wish to spend all their free time, and by whose opinions they measure all other persons and events.

These relationships are not always welcome to parents. The child's attachment to the best friend may challenge the parents' emotional hegemony; and even though the parents want their child to have friends, they may still unconsciously feel rejected when the child prefers spending time outside the family circle. In addition, a child often chooses as a best friend someone the parents don't really consider a "suitable companion," for any of a variety of reasons. But these best-friendships are an essential part of most people's friendship history, and the way the family reacts to them may set the tone for much of the relationship between parents and child through the whole adolescent period.

Flora's best friend, Hazel, lived next door. From the age of 8 they were inseparable friends—allies against the worlds of school and home. Flora recalls that this friendship gave her her first real taste of independence from what she was beginning to see as the limited world of her parents. Flora and Hazel spent long hours crouched in a little hideout at the bottom of the garden, talking endlessly about the feuds and passions of school life and the vagaries of their parents and siblings.

Flora's parents had many friends who were often in and out of their house, and they believed that the ideal was to have a large number of friends. Even though they knew that most children go through an intense best-friend period, they still wondered whether the girls were spending too much time together, to the detriment of other friendships, or becoming too emotionally dependent on each other. However, they kept these reservations to themselves.

When Flora was 9, her mother was invited to New Zealand for a year as a visiting professor. Flora felt the wrench from Hazel very keenly, and they carried on a sporadic correspondence. But when Flora came back, somehow she and Hazel could not recapture their former intimacy. Flora reluctantly moved into a wider, more complicated friendship world; she began having a series of best-friendships, each lasting a few months. This pattern was common among her classmates, and she remembers that it was useful to her in rapidly amassing intense experiences with many different kinds of people. But after age 18, Flora found that she no longer wanted this kind of all-encompassing friendship with just one person at a time. Her experience exemplifies the evolution most of us go through. Now, at 21, she says: "I prefer to spread my energy and enthusiasm among several close friends. That way I'm not overly dependent on any of them, I can be relaxed with them all, and none of us is too threatened by changes in our relationships."

By adolescence we have realized that our friends' families don't live the way our families do, and we begin to understand that their parents don't necessarily have the kinds of friendships our parents have. John's parents lived in a rural area, and their only friends were two other couples. They often visited each other on weekends and enjoyed quiet picnics or barbecues once or twice a month during the summer, but they never went out socially together. In John's experience, adult friendships consisted solely of sitting around at someone's house or talking at length on the telephone.

At age 14, John paid a summer visit to his cousin Tammy, who lived in a nearby city. Her parents were members of musical and theatrical groups and had many friendships which involved them in lively, unscheduled activities together—and, perhaps just as important, apart. Initially, Tammy's household seemed disorganized to John; he was upset when some spontaneous social event interfered with his usual dinnertime. Friends were always dropping by—for a drink or to plan a coming event or to pick somebody up for a rehearsal, a meeting, or a party. John had never imagined life could be such a whirlwind of activities. He also noticed that Tammy, her brother, and their parents all pitched in to keep the household running smoothly, though on a much more informal and irregular basis than he was accustomed to, given his own family's undeviating routine.

It had been so difficult for John to fit into this busy, energy-filled life that he returned home with a confused

sense of envy and loss, mixed with disappointment in himself and resentment at his parents. They had been, he
realized, loving and supportive in many ways—but why
had they not been able to give him an inkling that it was
possible to live in this open, friend-oriented manner? He
tried to find people in his hometown who lived more like
Tammy's family, since it was clear that his own family
lacked the outside interests that brought Tammy's family
into contact with so many interesting people. But it was
not until John went away to college that he was able to
establish his own new pattern of friendships, which were
not so chaotic as those of Tammy's family but which were
still far more active and spontaneous than those of his
own family.

If some parents fail their children by not providing
stimulating examples of adult friendships, other families,
especially those with authoritarian attitudes, actively attempt to inhibit adolescents' friendship experiments. In
such families, adolescents are given little room to be
themselves, to have opinions, to follow their own interests
and make their own mistakes—in friendship or anything
else. Rebellion is the usual result.

Bud remembers that his parents never really trusted his
choice of friends. During his adolescent years, his parents
were frightened by the fact that influences beyond their
direct control, such as TV and peer-group pressures,
offered behavior models that Bud found attractive despite
—or perhaps because of—their disapproval. Bud feels
that in his high-school years, he deliberately sought out
friends who would offend his parents. As he points out,
this worked both ways: he felt embarrassed by his parents' old-fashioned, rigid attitudes; and his parents were
mortified by his slovenly dress and semi-delinquent com-

panions. Once Bud narrowly missed arrest when one of his friends was picked up on a shoplifting charge. At this point, Bud began to realize that his parents had not been totally wrong to warn him that associating with some of his companions might pose real dangers to him. Although Bud didn't adopt his parents' views unreservedly and continued to resist their control in many areas, he did seek out some new and less antisocial friends.

Many of us can remember the mixture of resentment and gratitude with which we received the guidance our parents gave us about friendships they felt might be getting out of hand in the threatening areas of drugs, sex, or crime. Such advice has the best chance of having some effect if it is offered in a friendly rather than punitive way. But by the age of 17 or 18, children are on the verge of adult life, when they will freely choose their own friends, for better or for worse.

The early friendship history of many young people has been complicated in recent years by changes in American family patterns. Today, the husband is the sole wage earner in only about a third of all husband-wife families. Four out of ten wives currently work outside the home, and more than half of them do so by the time their children begin school. One in six families has only one parent, and more than half of these families are composed of widowed, separated, or divorced women and their children, or unwed mothers and their children. Two out of every five children born in the 1970s will spend some part of their childhood in a single-parent household. One marriage in four involves a man who has been divorced, and slightly more than one in four involves a woman who has been divorced. Both partners may bring into the new relationship children from a previous marriage or marriages, forming what social scientists have begun to call blended families. Children face the challenges of growing up in new, more fluid living arrangements, which may have some negative effects on them; but these arrangements also encourage independence and maturity, and offer children a greater range of models—in friendship as well as in other aspects of life—than the old patterns usually did.

Lee, who is now 20, grew up in a family situation that is not unusual today. His mother and father divorced when he was 7. When he was 9, his mother married a man who had two children from a previous marriage; he had custody of them during the year, and they spent summers with their mother. Lee recalls that his experience in the blended family was initially upsetting. He was suspicious of his new stepfather, jealous of his new stepbrothers, and secretly hopeful that his mother and father would reconcile. However, in time he realized that his stepfather gave him certain things that his biological father did not. The stepfather was more adventurous and brought a wider variety of interesting people into the house. He was also more emotionally open, which gave Lee the feeling that it was all right for *him* to express his own moods. And Lee made new observations about how men and women can relate, on the basis of the egalitarian relationship between his mother and stepfather. By the time Lee reached adolescence, he regarded his stepfather as a friend.

While difficulties between stepparents and children often arise, they generally seem to be only slightly more severe than difficulties between parents and their biological children, though stepparents may be resented more. However, a blended family, as Lee points out, can have the advantage of providing a richer than usual network of family connections. Lee, for example, became close to his stepfather's ex-wife's sister, who happened to teach science (Lee's favorite subject) in Lee's high school and in time became a sort of unofficial "aunt." His mother and stepfather had also retained friends from their previous marriages who visited the blended family household. This gave Lee an additional opportunity to observe an unusually wide variety of friendships.

Roughly one million unmarried heterosexual couples now live together, and about one in five such couples have children living with them, mostly from previous marriages. In addition, many gay couples live together, some bringing up children from earlier married lives. Such living arrangements may be somewhat less committed and durable than marriages, and children may feel threatened if they perceive the relationships as unstable. But we have noticed that from the children's standpoint, such arrangements provide valuable, complex learning situations, since couples who prefer to remain unmarried often maintain fluid friendship patterns that introduce a large number of people into the children's lives.

While these novel lifestyles may seem disconcerting, it is important to keep in mind that the traditional family, which supposedly offers its children a snug, secure nest in which to develop, is often a morass of tension, conflict, and feelings of psychic confinement, with consequent distortion of children's growth. The relationship patterns children learn in such environments do not equip them to relate in healthy ways as adults, either with mates or with friends. Gwen's family, for instance, did not provide the warm, intimate, emotionally nurturing environment that could have given her the confidence and trust in herself and others which make friendship possible. Gwen's mother had such fears and conflicts about intimacy that she had always kept her husband and daughter at a distance, and she socialized only when she was obliged to, exclusively with her husband's colleagues. Gwen's father, a moody, withdrawn surgeon who gave most of his emotional attention to his students, rarely spent time with Gwen, whom he regarded as his wife's responsibility. He made no secret of the fact that he bitterly regretted Gwen was not the son he had wanted. Gwen's childhood was isolated and unhappy, and left her with a crippling family friendship legacy.

When she finally left her hometown and moved to a large city, her attempts to establish meaningful friendships proved ineffectual. She would make overtures to people she met, mostly through her work, but these relationships never deepened; and soon Gwen would feel resentful and would withdraw. Gwen managed to counter her loneliness by starting a love affair with Ronald, a man she had met in her office. One evening, when she told Ronald about the painful ending of another abortive friendship, they got into a conversation about her early life. Ronald had sometimes been confused by what he saw as Gwen's vacillations between desire for closeness and fear of it, and he encouraged her to think about the patterns of relating that had prevailed within her family and in her parents' relationships with others. Gwen poured out her resentment of her mother and her rage at her father. She began to realize that her·parents' emotional shortcomings had set a pattern of interactions which made her feel both helpless and worthless—certainly not the kind of person others would naturally seek out as a friend.

Ronald's questioning and support helped Gwen see that she was repeating her parents' maladaptive relationship patterns in love and friendships alike. She resolved to try to extend to others the trusting feelings she had developed for Ronald and to take responsibility for reaching out to potential friends without grasping at them or expecting them to carry the whole burden of the relationship.

Brian was luckier than Gwen because he had a grandfather whose friendship model compensated for some of the deficiencies of his parents' friendship models. In fact, Brian says, if it wasn't for his grandfather, he would not have known what adult friendship was. His father was an airline pilot who was also involved in real estate, so his time was always over-scheduled. What little time he spent with Brian was mostly devoted to checking up on his progress in school and admonishing him to work harder. The family's social life revolved around real-estate contacts; and in Brian's experience, grown-ups' friends were people with whom they discussed business, over endless rounds of drinks.

But Brian's grandfather lived in an altogether different, friend-centered way. He was an opera singer who now appeared mostly in character roles. As a younger man he had made some lucky investments, so he had a modest but steady income that enabled him to work only during the opera season, though he did an occasional recording session. Thus, his time was quite flexible, and he devoted a good deal of it to Brian, his only grandchild, who also loved music. The grandfather's apartment was an easy bus ride away, and he encouraged Brian to drop in at odd hours and to stay over on weekends.

Brian's parents felt somewhat guilty that the grandfather gave more emotional energy to Brian than they did, but they were glad that the two were close. However, they didn't entirely approve of the grandfather's lifestyle. He rode a motorcycle and sometimes secretly took Brian for rides on the freeways, despite the parents' admonitions. He had a tendency to bring home interesting characters he met in stores or on the streets, some of whom Brian found rather bizarre. His grandfather's apartment was usually filled with musician-friends, and nobody made any attempt to conceal anything from Brian—so he heard all the backstage scandals, the backbiting and innuendo, sexual and otherwise, of the local music world.

The grandfather obviously enjoyed his friends enormously. Almost every evening he had people in for a vegetarian dinner, which he prepared and served with great flair. Brian noticed that his friends simply enjoyed each other's company and that nobody ever brought up business matters in any serious way. What really mattered to them was music; they talked about long-dead composers or singers as if they were still alive and old friends. Nobody seemed to care much about time: these companionable evenings often lasted until two or three in the morning, and Brian participated just as fully and to just as late an hour as any of the adults.

The grandfather respected Brian's talent and his opinions, and treated him as an equal. His friends, taking this as a cue, sometimes included Brian when they attended concerts. All in all, Brian feels that what he values most in his own adult friendships was learned from the free and joyful relationships he and his grandfather engaged in.

Our "family of origin" shapes and controls our friendship experiences throughout our early years. There comes a time, however, when we cut ourselves loose and, whether we are conscious of the process or not, begin to form our "family of choice"—the emotional support network of friends with whom we share a kinship of spirit rather than of genes.

As we approach adulthood and make increasingly independent living arrangements, we find that emotional bonds with our family of origin often become more tenuous, though we all remain linked to our families to some extent. If you are one of the rare people whose family of origin provided you with good friendship models, you will probably find it relatively easy to repeat those friendship patterns by choosing friends whom you wish to incorporate into your family of choice. On the other hand, if, like most of us, you come from a family of origin that provided insufficient or defective friendship models, you face the task of constructing or learning from others new patterns of relating which will enable you to select friends who can meet your needs.

Harold came from a large family and had never gotten along with his parents, who essentially had no friends. As he wryly puts it: "My original family had the unique strike against them that I didn't *choose* to associate with them. They had expectations I didn't want to meet, and I asked them for things they didn't want to give. I failed them, and they failed me." As soon as he was able to, Harold left home and stopped seeing his family in order to escape the constant parental pressures.

Once on his own, Harold saw that his family had failed to provide him with healthy friendship models. He also began to realize that relationships based on a mutual appreciation where unrealistic demands or expectations were not made on either side could fill the gaps left by his severed family relationships. Having felt unable to turn to his father or mother for disinterested advice, he became special friends with one person from whom he could seek counsel; but because he had been the youngest child in the family, to whom nobody paid much serious attention, he generally sought out friends who looked up to him as wise and experienced. Harold's family of choice thus consisted of people who accepted and liked him for who he was and with whom he could be himself.

Even if our family of origin provides us with good models for friendship with people like themselves, we may have initial difficulty relating to friends who come from different ethnic or cultural traditions. Rita, who comes from a large family, grew up seeing her parents relate to each other, their relatives, and their friends with great emotional intensity and close physical contact. In college, Rita became friendly with Phoebe, whose family life was characterized by emotional distance and personal reticence. Early in their relationship, the two women exchanged confidences about their families, friends, and men. Rita was genuinely curious about Phoebe and her life, and asked her a stream of questions. When she got to, "And what was it like when you made love for the first time?" Phoebe balked. "You're rushing me!" she protested.

Surprised, Rita asked what she meant. "Questions like that just feel intrusive," Phoebe replied. She explained that she didn't feel comfortable enough with Rita yet to talk about things like that. "And I've noticed that when I do tell you something intimate, you don't just listen. You're always jumping in with some opinion or telling me how you would have done it." Phoebe also felt that Rita touched her too much, considering the newness of their relationship; in short, she felt that Rita often infringed on her psychological space.

Rita replied that Phoebe sometimes seemed to be giving her the cold shoulder. "When you clam up on me, I can't tell if you really want to be friends. I wish you were more open and responsive. I hate it when you back off from me like that! Do you think we'll ever feel easy with each other?" Phoebe, remembering the pleasure they so often took in each other's company and particularly valuing their shared sense of humor, grinned and said: "Maybe we can take our differences as a challenge instead of an obstacle. I'm willing if you are."

As Phoebe and Rita got to know each other better, they compared childhood experiences. Phoebe began to see how her parents had consistently treated her in a cool, distant manner. Physical contact in the family was rare; personal questions were seldom asked, and if they were, they were couched in tentative and careful language. Phoebe also came to realize that her parents had dealt with their friends similarly. Rita, on the other hand, remembered many scenes when her parents had become involved in loud, emotional disagreements with each other or with friends, which were later followed by tearful reconciliations, hugs, and open declarations of affection. Such dramas had often been painful for Rita, but in her friendship with Phoebe, she was surprised to find she missed them: when she got angry at Phoebe, Phoebe would withdraw disdainfully instead of lashing back.

As their friendship deepened, they both made a deliberate effort to learn from each other's emotional repertoire. They came to re-evaluate the relationship models their families had given them, and they even developed a game of exchanging roles. When they went to a party, for example, Rita would try to act as if she had come from Phoebe's emotionally restrained family, while Phoebe would try to behave like someone from Rita's emotionally demonstrative family. Both still laugh about the first time they tried this. Rita made a firm resolve to keep her opinions and her hands to herself, to let people make overtures to her, and not to make overtures to them in her usual flamboyant way; Phoebe determined to push herself ardently into any situation that offered itself and to respond to everything said to her as if she'd known the person for years. As soon as they arrived at the party, they got into their assumed roles. By the end of the evening, Phoebe and a young British traveler had spilled out their whole life stories to each other and were drunkenly talking about eloping. Rita had spent the entire evening in a corner of the kitchen quietly receiving confidences from a poetic soul who finally said: "You know, I feel you *listen* to me better than anybody I've ever met. Maybe there's a future in this relationship."

Phoebe and Rita found such episodes hilarious but also curiously instructive. Playing the other's role in artificial party situations, they began to understand the advantages as well as the limitations of that role, and they also were able to see their own roles through the other's eyes. This kind of playful, half-teasing understanding brought them closer together without their having to insist that the other fulfill her family-induced expectations. In fact, this kind of exchange confirmed their friendship as being in some ways richer than friendships they had with people who were more like themselves.

Even in today's mobile, middle-class society, members of some large, closely knit families who remain in the same geographic area feel little desire to look outside the family for friends. Myra recalls that she had twenty cousins living within a few miles of her who saw each other frequently. The older generation encouraged this closeness, in fact, Myra's father once said to her disapprovingly: "Why are you spending time with that Betty? She isn't even a relative!"

But, of course, restricting yourself to friendships within even an extended family is, in the end, confining. Your adult family of choice must be broader and more varied than any family of origin can be. If you wish, you can later incorporate certain members of your original family into your family of choice. Generally, this happens with brothers, sisters, or cousins—family members of roughly the same age. However, serious effort is sometimes required to overcome the aftereffects of early family conflicts as well as to confront childhood modes of relating, which may have unconsciously persisted into adulthood.

Olivia had enjoyed being an only child and so bitterly resented the birth of her sister Maggie (who was born when Olivia was 6), as well as the births of her other younger sisters. Soon after the youngest child arrived, Olivia's father fell seriously ill and the family suffered great financial hardship. After that, Olivia remembers, there was never enough to go around—affection, attention, time, money, even food. As a result, Olivia left home as early as she could, supported herself completely thereafter, and for the next ten years saw members of the family only on occasional holidays.

Some years later, Maggie's husband and daughter were killed in an automobile accident, and her doctor suggested that a change of scene might help her get over the catastrophe. Maggie and Olivia had hardly seen each other for several years, so it surprised Olivia when Maggie called to ask if she could stay with her for a few weeks. Something about the way Maggie expressed her need to visit touched Olivia deeply; and putting aside her initial reluctance to open up old family wounds, she agreed to the visit.

The Maggie whom she came to know in the ensuing weeks was not at all the person Olivia remembered. To Olivia's astonishment, Maggie, even in her bereavement, displayed many of the qualities Olivia valued: practicality, good judgment, sensitivity, a willingness to be helpful, and a basic optimism about life. Slowly, Olivia came to admire Maggie for her ability to transcend the difficulties of their family background, as well as for her refusal to allow her loss to embitter her about life. Olivia realized with chagrin that she had always looked down on Maggie, yet now she decided that Maggie had shown more resilience in the face of catastrophe than she herself might have. This new respect, Olivia and Maggie both feel, was a crucial element in the shift of their relationship toward equality and friendship. It enabled them to clear up certain illusions they had had about each other. Maggie had thought of Olivia as superior, independent, disdainful of the family; however, she came to see that Olivia's attitude stemmed from her pain and disappointment over the reversal of the family's fortunes, which Maggie, being much younger, had not felt so keenly. Olivia had thought of Maggie as having it easy, continuing to live a smooth, stable life at home while she was out struggling alone in the world; however, she gradually saw that Maggie's dependence on the family, and the fact that she had married right out of it, had obscured her desire for experience and growth. Despite their differing life histories, both realized that their attitudes and perceptions were really quite similar. After years of misunderstanding and distance, they recognized that each was the kind of friend the other had always sought and that they belonged in each other's family of choice as well.

The similarities that can bind together members of a family of origin are strongest between twins, and the closest adult friendship we have encountered arising out of family ties is that between Francine and Alicia, who are identical twins. As Francine remarks, the two sisters had great empathy for each other as children, refraining from hurting the other, "since we knew *exactly* what the hurt would feel like." As they grew up, their experiences and friendships diverged somewhat. Francine married, had a child, and became a teacher; Alicia became a chemist. Although they retained an instinctive understanding of each other, as they matured, each came to represent something different in the other's friendship life. Alicia says she is the rational, sensible friend who balances Francine's emotionally turbulent friendships with her calm, businesslike perspective. Francine feels that she serves as an adventure-loving friend for Alicia, encouraging her to try new things and explore new friendships. Paradoxically, their own intimacy sets such a high standard that few friendships with others can equal it.

Parents and adult children sometimes like to think of one another as friends, and this is both understandable and admirable. However, realizing this objective is often hampered by such fundamental obstacles as generational differences in experiences and values. In addition, real friendship can develop only between people who feel roughly equal, and so long as children live at home, where the parents are, after all, in charge, this kind of equality cannot be achieved. Generally, such equality is possible once children have left home to live as they see fit, secure in their own values and lifestyle, and once parents feel sufficiently satisfied with the results of their parenting to relinquish control and allow the children to make their own decisions.

Earl and his son Chris, 23, had always been "pals," going on camping and hiking expeditions together. Earl says that he never condescended to Chris or implied that he lacked judgment, even when he was quite young. But it was not until Chris was on his own that the two began to see each other as friends. At this time, Earl was facing a professional crisis. He had applied for a new job, at a considerable increase in both salary and prestige. He had become so tense that he could hardly discuss the subject, even with his wife. One evening when Chris had dropped by the house, and he and Earl had had a few drinks together, Chris brought up the subject of Earl's anxiety about the job possibility. To Earl's surprise, Chris pointed out rather critically that inasmuch as Earl could only wait to see whether he in fact did get the job, it was pointless for him to make everybody else miserable in the interim. And it wouldn't be the end of the world, either, if the job didn't come through. Although Earl was startled to hear the sort of blunt advice from his young son that he would have expected only from an equal, he realized that Chris was simply manifesting his affection and concern. "He saw through my façade and challenged me, and I found I could take some pretty hard knocks without going down." Gratified that Chris was, in fact, quite perceptive about his father's limitations and weaknesses, Earl felt his life had been enriched by Chris's friendship and their ability to be open with each other about their feelings.

But the relationships between parents and adult children are always limited by the shadows of the past. Children never altogether forgive their parents for things they did or failed to do; and it is a rare parent who can deal with an adult child without memories of the child's former dependency sometimes imposing themselves. As Demetrios says, children tend to perceive their parents only in relation to themselves and not as people existing in relation to the world in general, with their own problems of family, love, and friendship. It had been very hard for Demetrios, an only child, to break the ties that had kept him living at home, despite offers of good jobs in other cities. He believed that his need for affection and approval could be met only by his parents; and he feared that they might withdraw their love or "die of a broken heart" if he disappointed them by striking out on his own.

Luckily, Demetrios's friend Wendell, who had faced a similar problem with *his* parents, told him: "Look, what you have to realize is that they're just ordinary, average people with ordinary faults and virtues and strengths. They won't die. They may even be proud of you if you strike out on your own. The important thing is that you do what you want to do, not what they want you to do. They aren't the only people who will ever love you, you know. There are millions of other people out there."

Wendell's down-to-earth advice helped Demetrios break out of his vicious circle of anxiety and need. He did, in fact, move to another city; his parents did not die; and he found that once his feelings of dependency on them had been diminished, his emotional energies were liberated. Not only did he fall in love and ultimately marry, but he was able to form several new and important friendships.

Unduly protracted emotional connections are not the only reasons why adult children choose to remain part of the family scene. Young people today, while still living at home, can enjoy a degree of sexual freedom that earlier generations felt they had to leave home to find. Adult children may also remain in the parental home until their mid-twenties because of the shortage of good jobs and the spiraling costs of college; and the incidence of early divorce may return them there in later years. However, it is usually difficult for parents and adult children living in the same household to coexist as friends. Parents often do not sufficiently communicate their own priorities in this middle stage of their lives. They may thus secretly resent the child's presence because it interferes with their plans to move to a different city or into a less demanding apartment or condominium lifestyle, to change occupations, or to seek further education. In addition, children may have trouble assuming the appropriate responsibilities, financial or otherwise; and the parents may be unable to relinquish their parental authority.

Bruce and his parents are an exception. Bruce has observed that his friends who live on their own spend all their available cash on rent, food, and car expenses; as a result, Bruce prefers to live at home. His parents have no objections to this arrangement provided Bruce bears his share of the mortgage payments, maintenance, and cleaning of the home. Even after meeting these responsibilities, Bruce has more cash and time on hand than do his friends. Because the needs and desires of both parties have been directly stated and are being met, Bruce and his parents have not only remained friendly, but they are in some ways becoming friends.

None of us can totally escape or deny the influences our families have exerted on our friendship patterns. Yet, we can and must—for the sake of our growth and sometimes our sanity—strive to recognize these influences. Our present friendships will almost surely benefit if we analyze our friendship history, tracing it back through adolescence and childhood, and confronting the issues raised. This knowledge can help us more clearly perceive the dynamics of our relationships and identify what past mechanisms are at work. Armed with such understanding, we might see that a friendship is merely a re-creation of an unsatisfactory childhood relationship and that it would be best to end it. On the other hand, we might realize, with pleasure and gratification, that the relationship is sustaining us in a way that our early friendship history has taught us to value highly, and so decide to explore it further.

Moreover, if we become parents ourselves, rethinking our own friendship history will better enable us to provide our children with a foundation for their friendship evolution. The most fundamental contribution we can make here is to establish a secure basis for our children's emotional growth and development. During their early years, we teach them, by word and deed, to trust others and to regard themselves as worthy of trust. We show them how to achieve intimacy and cope with emotional distance. As they get older, we must demonstrate to them that relationships are reciprocal; and if we have learned to interact spontaneously and playfully with our own friends, our children will learn, through their astonishing capacity for imitation, how to do so too. Only if friends are an integral part of our own family life will our children grow up naturally forming important friendships of their own, having learned the possibilities of adult friendships by observing them in action. This is the basic way in which we as parents can help our children understand that friendships are enriching, sustaining elements in life, the source of much of its joy and comfort.

3.
Mates and Friends

For most people, marriage* brings restrictions on friendship. An impending marriage often signals a redefinition
of friendship. Some friends fear that they will be seen
only when the domestic schedule allows it. Surprisingly,
the very friends who have the most to lose are often quite
accepting of this new peripheral role, perhaps because
they foresee they will do the same thing to their friends
when they form a committed relationship themselves.

Rebecca and Howard had been romantically involved
for two or three years, living in flexible, happy companionship with each other and their friends. They usually spent the weekend together and one or two evenings
during the week. When parties came up, they would go
either together or separately. Each had several close
friends from earlier years, as well as several they had
made together. Feeling that it would solidify their commitment to each other, Rebecca and Howard married.

They gradually began to focus their energies on their
new domestic life. Money they might once have spent on
social activities with friends now went toward the pur-
chase of new furniture. As Rebecca looks back on it, it
was as if some powerful myth of what marriage was *sup-*

---

* In this chapter, we will be dealing with marriage and marriage-like relationships; but to avoid terminological awkwardness, we will refer to all
stable couple relationships as marriages.

posed to be drove them in upon each other. This social pressure, combined with the natural deepening of their relationship, brought them to the point where they were tempted to think the world—and their friends—"well lost for love."

They soon began declining most of their friends' invitations and issued very few themselves. When they went out, to dinner or a movie or a concert, they preferred to be alone with each other. At first, their friends were tolerant, assuming that this exclusivity would be temporary. In time, however, the friends perceived that the condition was chronic. Although Rebecca and Howard would sometimes manage to find a few hours to spend alone with their friends, the friends would get the distinct impression that the quality of their relationship had changed. It was as if Rebecca and Howard would not—or could not—focus on or give themselves to the friendship in the way they had before. The friends began to call less often as their tolerance gave way to puzzlement, then anger, then resentment at the rejection.

The couple began to depend more and more on each other as they spent less and less time with their friends. Their feelings for each other, which had been quite equable, became extreme. Sometimes they would find themselves in a state of romantic intimacy, so close that they could hardly imagine ever needing anything from anybody else; at other times they would become intensely anxious at the possibility of losing the other. To their surprise and distress, their sex life, which had previously been joyful and relaxed, became erratic and unsatisfying. In addition, where once they had been able to go beyond their relationship to their friends, this was no longer an option; and they began to feel that their spouse was their only support and bulwark against the world.

A married couple's process of turning inward, which often is both unconscious and unnoticed by them, is one of the major threats to friendship. It is also a serious threat to the marriage. The expectation that any two people, however much in love, can totally fulfill each other emotionally is unreasonable; it also generates pressures which, in time, may well cause the marriage to collapse.

The relationship between Rebecca and Howard became increasingly troubled. Once or twice Rebecca made fitful attempts to reach out to her former friends. Not only was Howard antagonized by and resentful of Rebecca's overtures, but her friends, whose feelings were still raw, were not terribly receptive to her. The isolation of the marriage finally proved intolerable to Rebecca, and she moved out.

It took her more than a year to regain her former sense of independence, and she was unable to re-establish all of her old friendships. The lesson Rebecca drew from this was that it is precisely during the early, romantic years of marriage that people need to nourish their friendships in order to preserve them. Even when they are most deeply in love, she feels, people need others who can offer fresh perspectives on themselves and their relationship with their mate. She now sees that by allowing her friendships to wane when she married, not only was her own life impoverished but her relationship with Howard was deprived of the vitality that interaction with others might have lent it. She realizes that her friendships would have constituted a stabilizing force in her life and perhaps would have given her the resilience to cope with the difficult times most marriages encounter sooner or later.

Howard seems to have been more deeply shaken than Rebecca by the breakup and has never really regained his earlier faith in himself. He has been unable to rebuild his old friendships, and his new ones seem to be short-lived because of a growing drinking problem.

Although most married couples tend to withdraw from their friends, the withdrawal is seldom as extreme as it was with Rebecca and Howard. However, it is quite common in a less pronounced form; and it frequently puzzles Europeans, who do not expect from marriage the kind of exclusive togetherness that Americans often do. For them, it is natural for people who marry to maintain the separate friendships they had before marriage. We have observed that in more egalitarian marriages—those in which both partners work and pursue satisfying independent activities—American couples are developing this healthier pattern too. As Laurel, married three years to Frank, comments: "You may not spend as much time with friends after you've married, especially if you and your spouse are friends as well as lovers, but it's important to keep on sharing yourself with your friends." She has observed that marital intimacy (partly to her regret) has a way of overshadowing and displacing the intimacies that had previously prevailed between her and her friends. Once married, she felt linked with her spouse in a kind of "mutual protection association" that precluded many of the confidences friends customarily exchange. Thus, loyalty and a natural reticence about revealing intimate aspects of the marriage often superceded the former free and easy camaraderie.

Laurel is keenly aware of the contradiction here, and she and Frank have made a concerted effort to escape the national myth of couple togetherness, which assumes that aside from work and other necessities of life, a couple does everything together. Before they married, Laurel and Frank had interests the other didn't necessarily share. In many marriages, such interests are sacrificed in hopes that the couple will find common interests to enjoy together. But Laurel and Frank recognize that being married doesn't require giving up activities or people important to them. Instead of resentfully tolerating each other's separate concerns—which usually leads to their abandonment—they encourage each other's independent interests and the friendships that go with them. This is the only way, in their view, to integrate married life with a lively social life, so that it can draw energy from people outside, as well as from the couple themselves. Frank observes: "We feel more interesting—more like real-live people—if friends think of us as just two separate people who happen to love one another. If they start thinking of us as 'a couple,' something gets lost."

Frank and Laurel go so far as to recommend that if spouses don't have any separate friends their partners don't particularly enjoy, maybe they should find some! One of the functions of separate friends for married people is to help them maintain a strong sense of individuality, which many couples perceive as a key to preserving the excitement and mutual sexual attraction in their marriage.

Some couples who wish to continue seeing their separate friends may experience scheduling difficulties, which can easily make them feel that they are not seeing enough of either their friends or each other. Amanda and Christopher describe their "arrangement," which may seem a bit contrived to some but which worked for them. They initially set aside every Thursday evening as their "separate night out." They agreed not to make any joint plans for Thursdays and not to expect the other to participate, unless specifically invited, in anything they might do that night. Thus, they had some guaranteed "free" time in which to see friends, explore new interests not shared by the other, or do whatever they felt like doing. Once this agreement was made, neither of them felt trapped in a situation where they had to socialize together all of the time.

When people marry, they often try to incorporate separate friendships into the new couple relationship. Although there are times when this works easily and nat-

urally, more often than not either it proves impossible or
the consequences are painful. In any event, trying to force
such contact by insisting that the spouse spend time with
friends he or she doesn't like will only alienate spouse or
friend or both. And giving one spouse veto power over the
other's friends corrodes the mutual trust between the
spouses. It's best to recognize frankly that each spouse is
apt to have friends the other doesn't take to—or perhaps
even approve of.

When Sol and Stella married, Stella recalls: "I acquired
several instant friendships I really didn't want. I just
couldn't stand some of Sol's friends." Sol and Stella took
the best approach to salvaging the situation: Stella refused to get together with these friends; and Sol, who
knew that some of his friends *were* difficult, agreed to see
them separately. All the same, it has not been easy. One of
Sol's friends who has taken a great liking to Stella is still
trying to ingratiate himself with her—even to the point of
asking her how he should vote. Stella has accepted the
situation to some extent. "I still can't stand him, but at
least it gives me a double vote," she jokes.

Some friends are taken aback when they encounter
couples who have agreed to a marriage in which neither
has to see the other's friends unless he or she wants to.
These friends may be hurt by a spouse's decision not to
get together. Other friends may believe that, in principle,
married couples *should* always do things together; if they
don't, these friends may think the marriage is a rocky one.
Such expectations on the part of friends, relatives, and co-
workers unfortunately tend to make it more difficult and
more uncomfortable for couples to maintain separate
friendships without feeling apologetic.

The widespread tendency of Americans toward "compulsory coupledom" rests upon unrealistic assumptions.
Once they marry, two lovers accustomed to spending

their time with a number of single people may suddenly feel obliged to restrict their friendships to other married couples. Often enough, however, this flies in the face of the couple's real though sometimes unexpressed preferences.

While we shouldn't underestimate people's flexibility and generosity in doing their best to adjust to couple friendships, it is extremely rare for all four individuals in a two-couple friendship to be equally taken with one another. A certain amount of dissatisfaction is therefore inevitable in such groupings, and spouses often tolerate them at considerable costs in time and energy that they might have devoted to more satisfactory individual friendships. Without a strong commitment to continuing separate friendships, couples can become entangled in webs of frustration, as did Violet and Loren. Socially, they pursued friendships only with other couples. But when they spent time with Irene and Ralph, Ralph always drank too much and insisted on telling off-color jokes, which embarrassed Irene and irritated Violet and Loren, who would have enjoyed Irene by herself but couldn't conceive of seeing her except with Ralph. Ralph felt comfortable with Loren but thought Violet was a wet blanket; he might have enjoyed going out for a couple of drinks with Loren, but he too felt committed to the couple-to-couple pattern.

Violet and Loren had another pair of friends, Vince and Thelma. In this constellation, Violet was very fond of Thelma, who was an old school chum, but couldn't stand Vince because she thought he didn't appreciate Thelma. Loren liked Vince and thought he had a perfectly realistic attitude toward Thelma, who in his opinion tended to put on airs. Often after an evening together, Violet and Loren would say, "Never again"; yet when Thelma called with another invitation, they would somehow feel compelled to accept. However, their bitter arguments about Vince and

Thelma always focused on which of them was right, never on whether they should continue seeing the couple together or, perhaps, apart.

One factor that enables couples to make reasonably satisfying friendships with other couples despite the improbability of four people all somehow turning out to be close friends is that they allow a kind of "discount" for couple friendships. These relationships do not have to measure up to quite the level of intimacy or openness naturally expected of single friendships. Also, many couple friendships are found among people living in relatively traditional patterns, where business contacts between husbands often lead couples into socializing with each other. So long as the roles of both the husbands and the wives are fairly equal in status, such friendships may prove quite stable; but if one of the wives begins working outside the home, the delicate balance of relative equalities in the friendship may be disrupted, thereby endangering the couples' relationship.

We've observed that couple friendships are especially satisfying among "dual-career" couples, who face the sometimes overwhelming task of balancing the necessities of job, spouse, children, and household. They are justifiably reluctant to depend solely on the spouse for emotional support and companionship; and although they realize their need for the support that friendship brings, they often find that separate friendships are too time-consuming. Jerry and Maude, both busy professionals, with two children, thus deliberately establish friendships with other dual-career couples. Jerry says: "That way we avoid isolation, but we also get to see each other in outside situations, and we find we really enjoy the charge that builds up among four people who are interested in what they're doing."

.   .   .

Couples sometimes try to create other couples out of their single friends so that they can then relate to them in a couple pattern. This usually backfires. Sharon and Charlotte first met when they were in college. They lived in the same dormitory, studied in the same department, and appreciated the same sort of men. After graduation, Sharon married Sam, and he and Charlotte got along well. In fact, the three formed a three-way friendship of a familiar type, in which a couple may regularly include a single friend as part of their "family." This pattern was reinforced because Sam, who was a few years older than the two women, enjoyed playing the role of patriarch, which Sharon unquestioningly accepted at the time. Charlotte disliked this aspect of Sam's personality but found him so charming otherwise, and so interested in her welfare, that she tolerated it. He was, she remarked later, a good person to discuss problems with, and very sensitive, but "it was like talking to your father—it might be used against you later."

Sharon and Sam were happily married and hoped that Charlotte would find a satisfying love relationship, too. They made a point of introducing her to various candidates they found promising. Charlotte remembers wondering why they didn't just wait to see whom she might select; and in time she grew increasingly annoyed to find stray men dropping by Sam and Sharon's house whenever she was there. To Sam and Sharon's delight, she did become involved with one of these men; but as time went on, his reactions to emotional crises led her to feel he was insensitive and callous, and they broke up rancorously.

Sam and Sharon, however, did not share Charlotte's opinion, and they seemed almost to blame her for the breakup, as if she were the one who had disappointed their plans for a happy foursome. Worse still, Charlotte soon thereafter met Russ, with whom she began a serious relationship. She was looking forward to introducing Russ to Sam and Sharon, perhaps partly hoping to repay their many kindnesses by at last being able to relate to them as part of a couple. When they met, however, Sam and Sharon resented Russ because *they* hadn't introduced him to Charlotte; Russ, on the other hand, disliked the way Sam and Sharon related to each other. To Russ it seemed as if Sharon had lost her autonomy, adopting Sam's attitudes and even his mannerisms. It particularly irritated him that Sam continually said "We think" and "We like," assuming that Sharon always agreed. Russ later remarked to Charlotte that couples need to keep "I" a lively term in their vocabulary.

To Sam and Sharon's discomfiture, Russ and Charlotte not only proved to be a durable couple, but they eventually married. Although Charlotte tried to re-establish her separate friendship with Sharon once it became clear that the foursome would not work, Sharon so closely identified with Sam's views that it was awkward for her to see Charlotte so long as she was with Russ. The four now see each other only occasionally, at large parties.

Often when people marry, they become jealous or resentful of their spouse's old friends, especially friends of the opposite sex. We've been startled to observe how people who had easily accepted their lover's friendships suddenly became destructively possessive once they were married. Such jealousy can develop when the newly married people unconsciously fall back into early family dependency feelings and desperately cling to their mates the way they once clung to their parents. In the case of opposite-sex friends, such jealousy may have a specifically sexual component. But sometimes even people who have a solid sexual trust in each other may feel resentment that their spouse might prefer to share an evening with somebody else—even though they themselves may have no desire to participate in the evening's activity. Worry about gossip can be a factor here: a man may feel that if his wife enjoys the company of other men as friends, people will assume that there is something sexual in these relationships; a woman may feel the same way if her husband spends time with women friends. To combat potential embarrassment, the couple is wise to occasionally include these outside friends in joint activities, which will generally defuse the issue.

Sexual jealousy usually precludes couples from being friends with their former lovers; and some spouses, aware that jealousy may arise over even a nonsexual opposite-sex old friendship, will simply conceal the fact of that friendship from their mates. No one likes to lie, but no one likes to be subjected to unfounded jealous rages either. If one partner is convinced that the other partner is unable to accept such friendships, concealment may be the only possible alternative to abandoning the friendship.

When Linda married, her husband, Sidney, became very uncomfortable with Linda's continuing relationship with her old friend Clay. Linda and Clay had known each other for fourteen years; and although they were very close, there had never been anything sexual between them. Linda matter-of-factly assumed that her lunches and occasional after work drinks with Clay would go on, but to her distress Sidney became increasingly jealous. In time he became convinced, despite her assurances, that the friendship was, or at least must have been at some time, a sexual one. Though rather ashamed of his own jealousy, Sidney finally insisted that Linda stop seeing Clay. Feeling that not to do so would jeopardize the marriage, Linda finally acceded. This decision was especially painful for Clay, who observes: "If Sidney couldn't trust Linda and me, I don't know who he *could* trust! It was

just a terrible loss all around, and after fourteen years . . ."
Clay admits that he had suggested to Linda that they
could occasionally get together if she did not say anything
to Sidney. But Linda felt that she would be too uncomfortable with this breach of what she took to be marital
trust.

One spouse may become resentful of the other's outside
friends even when there is no real or even imagined sexual
element involved. Because people vary in their openness
to and need for friendships, prospective spouses should
ascertain whether they have sharply divergent views on
how much time and energy they will devote to friends,
both separately and as a couple. Some may feel it natural
to spend several evenings a week with friends, while others may prefer to socialize only occasionally. If such people marry, they face the difficult problem of arriving at an
acceptable compromise. Gil has a close "buddy" friendship with Louie, whom he had met one summer when he
was working on a ranch. Gil's wife, Margaret, believes
that Louie is, in a way, the brother Gil never had. Gil sees
it differently: he simply enjoys Louie's companionship.
When they go into a bar together, people gather around
to listen to Louie's stories. Louie's enormous enthusiasm
for life draws people to him, and Gil likes to share in his
gregariousness. Several evenings a week they make plans
to go out drinking together, and they always invite Margaret along. When Louie has a date with someone she
knows, Margaret sometimes accepts their invitations, but
in general she'd prefer to stay at home with Gil.

When Margaret first married Gil, she resented Louie's
demands on his time and, as she admits: "I worried that
Gil liked him a lot more than he liked me!" But as she got
to know Louie, she realized these fears were exaggerated.
Louie is very generous and often brings back little
presents for her from his trips. Margaret has come to
understand that the intensity of Gil and Louie's friendship

does not endanger her relationship with Gil, and she has stopped worrying that Louie will "lead Gil astray." Nonetheless, she is sometimes frightened by what she sees as Gil's need for other people. He seldom complains about her preference for staying home, but she feels he might come to believe he'd be happier with someone as sociable as he is. Gil loves Margaret, and he doesn't go out to escape her, but he cannot understand why she doesn't enjoy other people the way he does. Margaret has tried to cope with the situation by stating forthrightly to Gil what she needs: at least two or three quiet evenings at home, just with him and maybe a friend of theirs, but not a whole crowd. Gil has been able to accept this arrangement as the best solution to their differing friendship needs.

Louie basically understands Margaret's feelings and respects Gil's decision. Some single friends are not so understanding. If two women, for instance, have been friends for a long time and one of them decides to marry, the other may disapprove—not because she doesn't like her friend's prospective spouse but because she feels her friend has sold out the "blessings of the good single life" for a "craven need for security." Marriage no longer has the unquestioned moral superiority it once did, and such ideological objections to it have become fairly common.

On the other hand, if two men have been friends during their single years and both want to marry, the one who married first might incur the resentment of the other, who would still be languishing in his single state. Their friendship would probably suffer because of this resentment, as well as the diminished availability of the married friend.

While many married couples experience the problems we've been discussing, others like Laurel and Frank manage to integrate their friendships into a vital marriage partnership. It's a real joy when a person who has been the friend of one partner also becomes the friend of the other. It strengthens the friendship network and somehow reinforces the bonds of the individual friendships within it. In some marriages, the strength of the love relationship opens the partners up to friendship on levels they had not experienced before.

Tom, who grew up in the backwoods of West Virginia, remembers having four buddies throughout his childhood. Although they spent most of their free time together, Tom recalls they expressed their feelings only through neutral, "mechanical" talk—about guns and other objects, animals, projects. They did experience some emotional contact with each other through sports activities— the shared excitement of the game, the thrills of winning, the dejection of losing—but such things were never spoken about directly. All of Tom's teenage friendships dissolved after he left home.

Tom spent several years as a Peace Corps trainer in the tropics and then became a news photographer, traveling a great deal. For a year or so he had a friend with whom he shared many interests. Yet, the important things in the relationship—their feelings about each other—remained unspoken. As Tom now sees it, neither friend seems to have been aware that friends *can* discuss their relationship. By the time he was 30, Tom realized he had made no permanent emotional connections, and he felt that he would live out his life essentially alone, devoting himself to his work.

At this point, while on assignment covering a center for emotionally disturbed children, Tom met Marcia, a staff psychologist. As they worked together, Tom was impressed with Marcia's warmth and the obvious depth of her understanding of the children. Marcia was open with her own feelings about the often difficult circumstances of her work, but Tom said nothing about his own reactions to the center, to the children, or to her. One day she challenged him, saying: "Why don't you ever come out from behind that camera lens and share what you feel about all this?"

Something accepting about Marcia helped Tom respond. He began to pour out some of the pain and compassion he felt for the troubled children and—something he had not been conscious of when he began talking—his identification with the withdrawn, emotionally isolated children. Tom and Marcia began a sexual relationship, which proved powerful and compelling for both. Marcia felt that despite Tom's difficulty in talking about his feelings, he communicated with her sexually more fully than any man she had known. She says: "In some mysterious way, I felt understood and responded to—he was really there for me." After several months, they were married.

With Marcia's help, Tom began paying attention to his feelings and expressing them. Because he felt secure and loved, he found it easier to expose his feelings, both positive and negative. When something happened that pleased him, he made a point of saying so; when something upset him, he overcame his reluctance to let it be known. It was extremely hard for him to acknowledge—to himself or to Marcia—how much he wanted their relationship to continue and how threatened he felt by any thought of losing her. By doggedly refusing to allow feelings to go unresolved for long, Marcia showed Tom that people who love and trust each other can openly discuss what is happening between them with confidence that all will work out. Once Tom integrated this philosophy into his marriage, he was able to apply it in outside friendships. Hesitantly, he began to deepen the work-oriented relationship he had with a writer with whom he had often collaborated, by showing his own willingness to communicate his feelings, and he was pleasantly surprised when the writer responded in kind. Their relationship developed into a real friendship. As Tom recalls: "I felt I could ask for things and give things I never even knew were possible before." In time the writer also became a friend of Marcia's.

In time Tom found other friends. As he sees it, there was a kind of reinforcement between his marital experiences and these new friendships. A part of this was his discovery that having intimate contact with his friends gave him a valuable sense of emotional independence and strength in his relationship with Marcia and an unexpected sense of optimism about his future.

In remarriages, both partners are often in a better position to appreciate and participate in friendships than they were in their first marriages. Since four out of every five people who divorce will remarry (mostly other divorced persons), this is an increasingly important phenomenon. Both Bella and Stuart had been divorced for several years before they married. Bella says that she took her time, wanting to make sure Stuart was the right person for her. She wasn't infatuated with him as she initially had been with her first husband, but she knew herself better, had more confidence in her own experience, and was more emotionally secure. Stuart feels that by the time he married Bella, he had learned more tolerance and consideration; he found that he took her occasionally maddening idiosyncracies much more in stride than he had those of his first wife. Both Bella and Stuart feel they understand each other and are far more flexible and comfortable with each other than they had been with their previous spouses.

Bella and Stuart believe that people who remarry are especially attached to the friends who have stood by them through the difficult times of divorce, and they thus realize the importance such friends have for their new spouse after remarriage. As a result, they feel, remarried couples make a special effort to incorporate each other's old friends into their new social circle.

Many remarried couples, like Bella and Stuart, are not only some years older but somewhat better established professionally, and this allows and encourages them to take a serious interest in the spouse's work life and the friends connected with it. Such couples are also quite determined to pursue their own and joint interests, which often involve important friendship contacts. Stuart sighs: "Ah, if only we'd been able to learn all these things without having to be married the first time!"

Despite the many contradictions and tensions between marriage and friendship, many middle-class Americans unhesitatingly declare that their spouse is their best friend. Looked at realistically, this may more often be a goal than an achievement, but it indicates that people are striving to incorporate into their marriages the equality, mutual respect, regard for the other's feelings, and sense of independence they prize in friendships. This encouraging development seems to be relatively new, since real friendship between spouses presupposes fairly equal status and thus has become possible only as women have achieved more equality—both in and out of the home. It also presupposes a conscious priority on emotional candor and openness, which so far are chiefly aspired to in relationships among educated middle-class people.

These qualities, we believe, are equally necessary in marriage and friendship. A couple with a secure emotional relationship that is neither exclusive nor over-possessive has a model for each partner's dealings with friends. If the time you spend with friends seems flat or dull, consider whether the quality of attention you give them is comparable to what you give your mate. On the other hand, friendships can also provide inspiration for interactions with your spouse which have greater spontaneity, playfulness, and equality. Having a friend within the marriage, and close friends outside it, is an ideal not impossible for most of us to attain.

4.

Women's Friendships

Most women have traditionally defined themselves in terms of a husband and a family; and they've emphasized the nurturing, home-centered, noncompetitive side of their lives. Their self-esteem came principally from the approval of men, on whom they depended for both their economic security and their social position. Today, however, many women are rejecting such cultural mandates of how they should feel and behave. As they become aware of their own power, autonomy, and freedom to make choices, they are learning to value and develop their ability to grow intellectually, professionally, and economically; and in doing so, they are exploring new ways of living and loving. Like other aspects of women's lives, friendship patterns have also been changing rapidly; and as new choices of lifestyle, economic role, and social identity present themselves to women, supportive friendships with other women have become critically important.

Cecilia's marriage to Nathan had been going through hard times; even so, she was shocked when she awoke one morning to find the note he'd left by the toaster saying that he couldn't take it any more and that he'd be moving out once he returned from his business trip. Cecilia tearfully realized that she didn't know whom to call. Her parents were two thousand miles away; and besides, what would she say to them, and what good would their all too predictable response be? Her co-workers at the office had never become close friends with whom she could exchange important confidences; and the friends she shared with Nathan, she feared, might simply take his side, since most of them had been his friends before they were hers. She thought of several other possibilities but decided they were inappropriate: her old lover Dan, who had been so sympathetic to her problems in the past; and her college roommate, Adele, with whom she had communicated solely through Christmas cards for the past four years.

Rather to her surprise, Cecilia ended up confiding her marital disaster to Grace, a neighbor she didn't know very well but who had been helpful once when Cecilia's car battery went dead. It turned out that Grace herself had been divorced and could identify with Cecilia's predicament. Grace was not only sympathetic and supportive, but she also had practical advice to offer. Cecilia, she pointed out, had made the common mistake of depending on one person—her husband—to fulfill her needs for companionship, intimacy, and emotional support. Grace told her: "Putting that kind of emotional burden on one relationship is always dangerous. If you don't have your own friends, you're totally vulnerable if anything goes wrong with that relationship." Grace had analyzed Cecilia's situation correctly. Cecilia had failed to develop and maintain a support network of friendships, with women or men, independent of her marriage. Like many other people who find themselves alone because of separation, divorce, or a spouse's death, Cecilia realized she had no real friends of her own. Encouraged by Grace's example and counsel, she slowly began to establish new friendships and to renew several former acquaintanceships she had never developed. She also resolved that whatever happened in her romantic life, she would never again deprive herself of the sustaining friendships whose value she had come to appreciate.

Whatever a woman's emotional and sexual involvements with partners may be, she must meet her basic needs for emotional contact and understanding at least partially through relationships with friends. Women who raise children alone, whether they are separated, divorced, or widowed, have been finding that if they share their life with other single parents, the experience can be sustaining and rewarding for all concerned, though not without difficulties. Claire and Joanne, both divorced, met by chance when their children were very young; they happened to rent apartments upstairs and downstairs from each other. Claire, who was British, had left her husband in New England and come to Chicago to start a new life, bringing only her two children and a regular child-support check. Joanne had lived in Chicago since her student days and also had a very young child.

Claire disapproved of Joanne's loose supervision of her daughter, Poppy, whom she allowed to swear and freely express disagreement with adults. Joanne was surprised at Claire's insistence that her children address adults as "Mr." and "Mrs." and remain quietly at the table until excused. Neither would have predicted they could ever tolerate each other, much less become friends.

In time, however, proximity brought the two women together despite their different approaches to child rearing. Since their apartments shared an enclosed backyard where the children—now ages 4, 5, and 6—could play together, they could take turns watching them and gain a freedom of movement that few single parents can manage —a critical need for single parents who also work, even part-time, as Joanne and Claire both did.

Joanne and Claire gradually came to understand each other's ways and manners and rhythms. Joanne was a gregarious person who loved company. She had regular lovers, and for a time one of them lived with her. Claire was a solitary person who preferred to keep much of her time for reading and painting; and she went through long periods when she had no sex life at all. Joanne learned to be comfortable with Claire's need for privacy; she knew that when she had friends over for supper, Claire might be willing to join them just for dessert and coffee, although she would rather interact with friends on a one-to-one basis.

The two women shared a vigilant independence: both had left limiting marriages to devote themselves to developing their individual talents. Claire began to experiment with sculpture; Joanne finished her Ph.D. and began a book. Rather to their surprise, they found they could discuss these creative interests in depth with each other over a comforting cup of tea. Claire was often anguished about the uncertainties she faced in her art, which demanded an attention and commitment that sometimes made her feel out of touch with normal life. Joanne, endlessly writing and rewriting, sometimes felt that the more she learned, the less able she was to compress it into readable prose. In time they realized that they could trust each other's judgment and advice about their work as truly disinterested, requiring no secret discounting. Claire, Joanne discovered, was really not a moralistic person and could be counted on for cogent, strong-minded advice about Joanne's tumultuous love life or the perils of academic politicking. And Joanne, with her sturdy go-ahead pluck, helped Claire out of her fits of creative depression and isolation. They gradually learned to read each other's movements, facial expressions, and thoughts; and sometimes they even joked about "getting married and looking for a house together."

Remarkably, the fact that Claire had never learned to

like Poppy, a headstrong, uncontrollable child who often pitted Claire's children against each other, did not undermine the friendship between the two women, though Poppy meant the world to Joanne. Both women were perfectly aware of the other's feelings, but they managed never to confuse their feelings about Poppy with their feelings about each other, so their mutual allegiance was never endangered, though this aspect of their relationship was a source of pain for both.

Claire and Joanne's family-style friendship has sustained them and their children for six years with a firmness equal to that of most contemporary marriages. In fact, the understanding and trust of their friendship surpass those of all too many marriages, and it is naïve to consider such relationships a second-class substitute for marriage.

There has always been a tradition of young unmarried women living together. In college or shortly thereafter, they have often teamed up with friends to assure themselves of companionship and support, to share an apartment or house too expensive for them to afford alone. Today such arrangements are still prevalent, and they have also become popular among people in their thirties and forties, as a result of conviction as well as necessity. Some women have decided against marrying or having children. Others, who are separated, divorced, or widowed, find themselves without sufficient resources or job skills to provide an adequate income. Like many women who have never married, they are aware that in crises of illness or accident, most of their friends who are involved in families or other emotional commitments will be able to lend only limited support. But, as Claire and Joanne's experience shows, much of the kind of comfort a woman gets from a spouse can be obtained from a friend who is also a long-term living companion. Moreover, women are becoming aware that there may be emotional and physical hazards associated with living alone: single, divorced, or widowed women have higher rates of mental illness, are more likely to commit suicide and to have higher accident rates and rates of serious diseases than married women. It is likely that living in a family or family-like situation can reduce the incidence of these hazards as people look out for each other's health and well-being, and satisfy each other's emotional needs.

It is among older people, particularly older women, that the need for sharing is most pressing. In the over-65 age group, 70 percent of the men are married as compared with only 30 percent of the women. This can be attributed to the fact that women on the whole live somewhat longer. Some older women do not wish to remarry or live with a man; however, their need for companionship persists. At the same time, their incomes often cannot accommodate a single-dwelling lifestyle. For these reasons, there seems to be a growing tendency among women who have been friends to consider living together in their later years.

Two teachers, Rosemary and Deborah, had been good friends for almost thirty years. They began teaching at the same school in the same year and thus shared the difficulties of adapting to a new work situation. They weathered the school's discipline problems, budget cuts, declining test scores; they saw principals come and go; but they remained—veterans of the educational wars. They lived within a few miles of each other most of this time and socialized together regularly, both separately and as couples. Neither had children. Rosemary's husband died very early, of cancer, and she never remarried; Deborah's husband was killed in a car crash when she was 55. Shortly thereafter, Deborah began to consider an early retirement and discussed with Rosemary the possibility of their joining forces and moving to Florida, where they had happily vacationed many years before. Rosemary worried that she was "too set in her ways" to live with anyone else but agreed to go on a ten-day expedition. As it happened, the two women ran into several retired teachers who made them feel at home in the area, emphasized how pleasant life there was, and promised to help them get established.

Though both Rosemary and Deborah were naturally hesitant to make such a large commitment to each other, they finally decided to take the plunge. They retired, sold their houses, and moved into a solar heated beachfront cottage on the Florida coast. Their many shared interests and tastes helped minimize the frictions of living together, and they found they very much enjoyed the steady comfort that came from the other's presence. Gradually, they became involved in community and church activities, which took up some of their time; and their new friends helped them enlarge their circle of acquaintances. They report, three years later, that their new life has been so mutually rewarding and satisfying they would never live alone again.

As women's changing roles and lifestyles present new and exciting possibilities, the process of adjustment may stir up conflicting feelings about traditional values and attitudes. Though change is necessary and will in the end benefit both men and women, it may initially cause varying degrees of pain, depression, and anxiety.

Patricia and Lisa had gone through college together and lived in the same neighborhood for several years afterward, spending a great deal of free time together. Then Lisa decided to do graduate work in biology. Suddenly, she had considerably less time to spend with Patricia than before; and during exam periods, she had no time at all. This hurt Patricia's feelings despite her understanding, as a professional herself, that it was important for Lisa to pursue a career she thought would be rewarding. Yet she hesitated to bring the matter up. She also found, to her surprise, that she began to feel jealous of the new friends Lisa was making through her graduate school contacts; and to confuse matters still further, Patricia could see that the demanding experiences of graduate school were making Lisa more lively and assertive, and that her interests were shifting away from the easygoing, leisurely pursuits she had once shared with Patricia. Patricia comments: "Lisa seemed to be turning into a different person. I liked and admired some sides of the new Lisa, but the process was really unnerving. I worried that we might be growing apart in ways that could end our friendship."

Patricia had invited Lisa to a chamber music concert and was looking forward to a relaxed evening of sharing music they loved. Just as Patricia was about to leave the house, Lisa called to cancel, saying that she simply had to finish an experiment on which she'd been working. Suddenly all Patricia's feelings of anger, resentment, and jealousy spurted out. To her astonishment and shame, she found herself shouting at Lisa about how disappointed and betrayed she felt. Lisa was very upset at the depth of Patricia's wounded feelings. She explained as carefully as she could that she too regretted very much that they didn't have as much time to spend together as before. "Maybe I'm a more matter-of-fact person," she said, "so I've just accepted it without giving it too much thought, and I've been *so* busy that I've hardly had a moment to myself either." Patricia was mollified by Lisa's sincerity and comforting reassurances. She said that probably one of the reasons she was so angry was that she was in a rut with her own work, had a lot more time on her hands, and envied Lisa's commitment to her new career. They both knew it was important for their friendship to talk the matter over further, so they made a date for later in the week—which Lisa scrupulously kept. They discussed their feelings and attitudes about their friendship and discovered that neither of them had fully taken account of the changes in it: Lisa had not realized the degree to which she had limited the time she spent with Patricia, and Patricia hadn't appreciated the extent of Lisa's investment in her new endeavors. Once they saw the new situation clearly, they both felt they could relate comfortably within it, and their relationship again felt sound and secure to both of them. Patricia also resolved to spend more time with other friends as a way of filling the gap left by Lisa's absence. As time went by, these relationships grew more important to her, and she felt she had come to a good compromise about the amount of time she spent with Lisa and with others.

A major contribution of the feminist movement has been its attempt to bring women together, through women's groups and other women-oriented activities, to share and explore the pain as well as the exhilaration of change. Patricia and Lisa were fortunate that they could confront their problem honestly and ultimately come to terms with it before it destroyed their relationship. But many conflicts are far more complex and difficult to resolve, and women often find it helpful to discuss their problems with women whose experiences may parallel their own and who have a strong interest in encouraging their openness and growth as individuals.

The atmosphere of such women's groups is usually

strongly supportive and anticompetitive, a spirit aimed at countering the traditional notion that women can never trust other women because they are all in competition to "make a good catch." In the past, such competition was, in fact, real and very understandable, since women's economic dependence on men forced them to put such considerations above loyalty to and friendship with other women. But as women have achieved greater equality and economic independence, the notion of them as unscrupulous competitors for men has begun to die out. At the same time, women who enter the professional world will have to be competitive—for power, status, and money—not only with men but with each other, just as men are competitive with other men. Women's sexual mistrust may thus give way to a new mix of assertive competition for individual rewards and supportive concern for all women.

Despite their competitiveness, women in our society appear to have had a great capacity for making and keeping close women friends. This may be due, in part, to the fact that traditional housekeeping and child rearing involved much nonstructured time spent in the company of other women who shared similar concerns. In addition, female children have been encouraged to be emotionally expressive, and this may further contribute to women's capacity for intimacy.

Only women can truly understand other women in terms of certain biological aspects of their lives: menstruation, pregnancy and childbirth, and breast-feeding. A special bond is created between women who share these experiences, experiences which their mates can never fully participate in. These bonds often lead to friendships when the women are in their twenties, the average time of childbearing, though there is a growing tendency to postpone childbearing until the late thirties and early forties.

Friendships built around motherhood have been particularly meaningful for Laura, who until then had had no real women friends. Laura's field was engineering, and all her fellow students and colleagues had been men. Her limited contact with women had led her to assume that she was simply not adept at relating to women, with whom she had no shared interests and experiences. It was not until she married and had her first child that she made any important emotional contact with other women and started developing the friendships she still has today.

During her first pregnancy, Laura discovered that Melissa, a former neighbor, had gotten married and had become pregnant at about the same time Laura had. Both women were interested in having natural childbirth, so they attended exercise training classes together, encouraged each other to get their husbands involved, and helped each other prepare for the births and the babies' first difficult weeks. After the babies were born, Laura and Melissa (who had both chosen to assume the major childcare responsibilities while their husbands assumed the major economic responsibilities) spent much time together visiting, shopping, going out with their babies in strollers, and, when the children grew older, bringing them together to play. Laura and Melissa shared both the delights and the day-by-day miseries of the early childhood years.

Through these experiences, Laura learned that she was capable of sharing important concerns with women and that she could respect and admire women friends as much as she had her men friends.

This process was repeated with another woman when Laura became pregnant again some years later; and during her third pregnancy, which was very difficult because of medical complications, Laura met Jennifer through the La Leche League, an organization promoting breast-feeding. As it turned out, Jennifer had a premature delivery. The two were thus able to share the anguish and uncertainty of their circumstances, and they became close through their parallel situations of stress and crisis.

Thus Laura, who still maintains friendships with all three women, gained a friend with each child, in a sort of cascading pattern. Her rewarding experiences with these women led her to feel that reaching out to women in other circumstances might also be enriching. As she embarked on new friendships with professional women in scientific fields related to engineering, she discovered that these women were also struggling to overcome the effects of role stereotyping, which had kept them from relating seriously and equally to other women.

Women who work full-time can no longer have traditional home- and child-centered friendships like Laura's, and their work life does not really provide emotionally equivalent friendship possibilities. It's no surprise, then, that women have become conscious of the need to develop new types of support networks. The feminist movement has made a significant contribution in this direction by stressing that friendships with women can be as emotionally valuable and rewarding as love relationships with men, though of course the satisfactions of such relationships are different. Honesty and candor in communication, which are essential to full mutual understanding and acceptance, make possible a closeness in friendship which traditional friendships seldom attained. When women have experienced such openness with other women, they may well seek to relate more deeply and honestly with the important men in their lives.

In recent years, women have been especially adventurous in exploring new friendship patterns and possibilities. For example, though most friendships involve two people, we encountered a three-person friendship in which a conscious attempt had been made to break out of the pair pattern. Vera and Claudia first met through political work in the feminist movement. What attracted them to each other was that they shared a Mediterranean warmth of character: they were both intense, emotional, sympathetic people who were quick to condemn and equally quick to forgive. Even in their disagreements, which were frequent, they felt comfortable with each other, and they began to work together regularly on feminist projects. They also found that they complemented each other. Claudia, a dancer, was more attuned to feelings and the psychological ramifications of events, whereas Vera tended to focus primarily on ideas and how to structure and implement them. Their differences stimulated them to attempt projects they might not have undertaken alone.

Vera and Claudia met Alix when she approached them for interviews to be used in a book she was writing. They were drawn to her by the way she combined insightful questioning with a wry sense of humor; she had a kind of quiet equilibrium that intrigued them and that felt both stimulating and supportive. Moreover, the three of them realized that they had a very similar political approach, with many overlapping tastes and values. As Vera says, they were "California feminists, interested in changing life patterns rather than waving placards."

As the months went by, Alix crossed paths with Vera and Claudia more and more frequently. Alix's equable nature reassured the two women that if the three became close friends, she would preserve a balance in her affection for them both. They thus actively opened their friendship to her, and their common interests in feminist work cemented the three-way relationship. Their delight in simply being with each other also inspired them to plan feminist projects they could carry out together: Vera and Alix wrote a book; Alix and Claudia wrote articles; and the three started a feminist film producing and distributing company. More and more, they realized that there was strength in their diversity: Claudia, as the others saw her, was "more subtle"; Alix had a strong sense of drama; and Vera was a galvanizer and critic.

Over a period of several years, the three women remained close. Claudia found an apartment near Vera's, where Alix also spent a great deal of time, and their lives became intertwined on an almost daily basis. By this time, they had become aware that the three-way quality of their relationship was important and precious—and they also realized that it had to be nurtured and protected, for it could easily have been thrown off balance and split. They saw that there were various lines of potential cleavage of which they had to be cautious: there was an age difference between Vera (44) and Claudia (41), and Alix (33), which made communication between the two older women easier in some respects; Alix and Claudia lived by themselves and had no children, while Vera had a husband and two small children; and Alix and Vera were more immersed in the feminist movement than Claudia was. But these pairing tendencies never threatened the overall solidarity of the trio. As Alix puts it: "We wouldn't jeopardize what we all had together." Above all, they learned that it was crucial to keep the lines of communication open so that whenever problems arose, they could be dealt with swiftly. In time, they developed what they now look back on as a kind of "family feeling."

When discussing their relationship, these women point out that from a radical-feminist viewpoint, such friendships have particular advantages. Pair friendships, they maintain, whether between a man and a woman or between two women, duplicate some of the oppressive features of the traditional man-woman couple. The women also argue that society's emphasis on "coupling" has been a way of controlling and oppressing women, keeping their commitments narrow and discouraging them from exploring emotional possibilities with a variety of people. Thus, the experience of a three-way friendship not only gives women the kind of support they need to become less dependent on lovers or husbands, but it also presents a kind of model for women's relationships in general.

However, they have also discovered that when three people are friends, an argument or profound difference of opinion between two of them is very painful for the third as well. The third friend, who is used to relating intimately and directly with both of the others, suddenly finds it necessary to stand aside and withhold comment, since anything said may be interpreted as supporting one side or the other. This objective stance is the only way the third friend can avoid feeling disloyal to either or possibly both. All a third friend can do in such a situation is to emphasize plainly the affection held for both parties and the importance of their resolving the conflict. Such a conflict may eventually cause the three-way friendship to dissolve, although the individuals may continue to see each other separately.

A three-way friendship, if it remains balanced, has benefits no two-way friendship can enjoy. Each friend brings out different facets of the others, so that in their interactions as a group there are complexities and subtleties which no two of them, interacting alone, could experience. Alix, Claudia, and Vera were very conscious that this kind of enrichment increased the fascination and delight they felt for each other. Because people are limited by character and background, they cannot bring out in others everything that is there. Often, these unexplored possibilities remain "invisible" until they see those friends interacting with someone else—and thus they can appreciate aspects of their friends which they themselves could never evoke, however intimate their friendship might be.

The past decades have witnessed a substantial broadening of possibilities for sexual expression. Not only do many young women no longer feel constrained to be monogamous, in or out of marriage, but bisexual and lesbian relationships have become more widely accepted, at least in metropolitan areas. This new sexual freedom, however, has created situations for new kinds of ambiguities and misunderstandings to develop between friends.

Jackie and Carolyn described an experience they had which demonstrates how easily confusions can now arise regarding the sexual intentions even of close friends. Jackie notes that in the past, touches between men and women were normally interpreted as tentative sexual signals, and touches between women remained highly stylized (a kiss on the cheek, a pat on the arm) and were uniformly assumed to be nonsexual. But today, as Jackie puts it: "You can't always be sure you know what's going on!" Carolyn agrees that new sexual attitudes can frighten women like herself, who seek closeness with other women yet do not want to become sexually involved with them.

Jackie and Carolyn had been friends for seven years. Carolyn, who was herself divorced, had helped sustain Jackie through a painful divorce. They set up a women's group together and saw each other frequently. They had a good understanding; and when they were together, they related intensely and greatly enjoyed the intimate discussions they had.

Even among women like Jackie and Carolyn who know

each other so well, trust each other implicitly, and are well aware of the other's solidly heterosexual orientation, a panic over the possibility of lesbian contact can arise. Carolyn eventually became deeply involved with Bill, and Jackie of course came to their engagement party. A great deal of champagne flowed, and several guests ended up having too much to drink, among them Jackie, who got rather sloppy and affectionate.

When Bill sat down on the couch beside her, she threw her arm around him, and the two chatted for a while in a cozy fashion. Then he went off to open more champagne and Carolyn sat down in his place. Jackie threw her arm around her, too. As Jackie gesticulated, telling some of the lively, funny stories that endeared her to Carolyn, her hand, hanging down over Carolyn's shoulder, grazed Carolyn's breast several times.

Suddenly, Carolyn became conscious of Jackie's hand against her. She found herself wondering what that hand was doing there. Was Jackie conscious of its brushing against her breast? And why had she even noticed it? Why was it upsetting her? Her joy in the engagement party quickly evaporated, and her heart sank. Was Jackie, inebriated as she was, revealing some sexual feeling that had never before surfaced? Or was she herself being ridiculously suspicious and over-sensitive? After all, they had often seen each other nude in hot-tubs or sunbathing, had often given each other warmly physical hugs. So why was she so worried? Her whole body froze, and she decided to get up, on some pretext, to escape the situation.

Later, when Jackie had left, Carolyn told Bill what had happened and described her feelings about it. She asked whether he thought Jackie could have meant anything sexual, and he assured her that from his observations, Jackie was simply too drunk to have noticed what her hands were doing. Carolyn, after some days of reflection, concluded that he was probably right, but she was still disturbed to see how upset she had been. She was an advocate of gay rights and had several bisexual and lesbian friends, yet here she was, worrying whether this incident would somehow completely change the nature of her relationship with Jackie.

A few days later, when the two women got together, Jackie was apologetic for drinking so much and said she couldn't remember anything after the cutting of the cake. Carolyn said there was something she needed to check out with Jackie and described the incident, sharing the conflicting feelings it had raised. Jackie was surprised because she was totally unaware of having touched Carolyn's breast in a way that could be considered the least bit sexual; she remembered simply feeling affection and happiness for Carolyn in a relaxed and easy way. But she said that she could understand Carolyn's feelings and was glad Carolyn had mentioned them, so they wouldn't get in the way of their friendship. She assured Carolyn that warm as her feelings were for her, she had no desire or intention to express them sexually, and she knew that Carolyn felt the same way. They talked about how hard it is for women today to distinguish between physical contact that is supportive, nurturing, and affectionate, and physical contact that is sexual. Carolyn was relieved, and Jackie was deeply pleased that Carolyn trusted their friendship enough to bring up such an awkward topic. After their discussion, they gave each other a hug, laughed, and felt the problem had been comfortably resolved.

Women's friendships, like men's, can last a lifetime if they rest on a solid foundation and remain flexible enough to adjust to life's changing circumstances. Jeanne and Kathleen have maintained a friendship for more than twenty years. Now in their late thirties, they met in 1958 in a Midwest college literature course, where they discovered their mutual fascination with contemporary poetry. This shared interest linked them in a sort of pact against their unimaginative fellow students and the good, small-town backgrounds from which both had come.

Jeanne, whose father was financing her education, admired Kathleen for supporting herself, through a library job and a scholarship; Kathleen's father had died when she was 12. Kathleen admired and envied Jeanne her carefree attitude and bubbly good humor.

During their senior year, they rented an apartment together off campus. They considered themselves best friends, but, as many women did in that period, Jeanne thought nothing of breaking a date with Kathleen if a last-minute invitation came in from a man. Jeanne's first priority, she frankly admitted, was to find a husband. Kathleen, on the other hand, increasingly enjoyed the intellectual stimulation of research; her shyness and her determination to maintain her scholarship by getting good grades prevented her from having more than occasional dates, despite Jeanne's attempts to introduce her to many of her men friends.

In time, Kathleen graduated with honors and received a fellowship to graduate school. Jeanne fell in love with Preston, married him, and moved to the suburbs, where he had a job in an electronics firm. As Kathleen looks back on it now: "During this period I envied Jeanne's financial and emotional stability. But I felt she was paying a higher price than I would be willing to pay. She got very caught up with her two children, and we saw much less of each other, especially because I had the feeling Preston didn't much like me. But there was no question that we were still friends—in fact, best friends."

Jeanne remembers that she admired Kathleen's adventurousness in pushing her way into a male-dominated field. "But I worried," Jeanne admits, "that Kathleen was making too many sacrifices for a far-off professional career. I guess I also envied her affairs, though she never seemed to be able to maintain a stable relationship for long and she never thought about having children." Both secretly felt that the other's adjustment was so fragile that honest questioning of it might prove catastrophic; they never openly addressed each other's basic life choices.

But Jeanne began to feel confined in her isolated suburban house with her small children. One day when Kathleen had come to visit her, Jeanne took a deep breath and revealed that her sex life with Preston was practically nonexistent and that she was often overcome by feelings of marginality and uselessness. She confessed that she wished she were more like Kathleen, whom she had once called Wonderwoman, struggling along out there in the real world. Kathleen confided that things hadn't turned out as she had hoped, either. She had been passed over for promotion in her department because she was a woman, and she worried that she would be unable to find another position because the bottom was dropping out of the liberal-arts field. In addition, her love affairs tended to end inconclusively, and she had begun to wonder if she would ever combine love and work.

In this conversation, the two women really leveled with each other about their feelings and ended up expressing their mutual relief that they had been able to share their misgivings and pains. Instead of such revelations alienating them as they had feared, they drew the two women closer together.

Shortly thereafter, Jeanne left Preston and moved back to the city with her children. Her fascination with the development of her children had interested her in the effects of social problems on children, and she decided to train as a social worker for delinquents. She and Kathleen resumed spending much of their time together, now on a more frank and open basis. They know their friendship is bound to go through many more changes, but they are confident that it will endure. Kathleen recently ran into a man she had known earlier as a teaching assistant, and they are now married. They work hard at their professions, share their domestic duties equally, and have no plans for children. As Kathleen told Jeanne with a laugh: "At last I've managed to combine passion and productivity!"

5.

Men's Friendships

In recent years, a great deal has been written about men's and women's different modes of relating to the world and to other people. Extreme positions have been taken on the hypothetical roots of traditional friendship patterns. On the one hand, some male writers argue for the existence of a unique bond of cooperative friendship among men, supposedly derived from the life-or-death cohesion of prehistoric hunting bands or warfare groups. This innate capacity for bonding allegedly explains modern man's capacity for teamwork, which enables him to establish and operate governments and corporations, to compete in group sports, and to wage war. On the other hand, some female writers argue that women have an innate capacity to form nurturing emotional bonds of intimate friendship with other women, perhaps derived from their common biological experience of childbearing and child rearing.

These dramatic but speculative arguments, unfortunately, are sometimes used to downgrade the other sex's friendship capacities. This is counterproductive to a useful understanding of the differences that do exist between the traditional patterns of men's and women's friendships. Moreover, such arguments tend to imply that genetic shaping forces may be at work. But male and female children are socialized so differently that it is unnecessary to invoke biological programming to explain why they exhibit different friendship patterns as adults.

Women's friendship networks tend to be strong at the center: most women relate intensely and intimately with several close friends they see frequently. Women's relationships with other women positioned along the outer edges of the friendship network tend not to be focused on practical projects and generally lack a utilitarian side. Men's friendship networks, on the other hand, tend to be strong and sharply defined in the outer areas, where relations are seen in terms of function and purpose more than in terms of feeling—business friends, sports friends, hobby friends—and weak in the central area: many men have few or no friends with whom they relate in an emotionally open and trusting way and without some kind of practical agenda.

In contemporary society, friendship patterns between men and women have begun to converge. Women critical of their traditional training are seeking to develop mutual support habits, through business teamwork and organizational skills, in order to build more structure into the outer parts of their friendship networks; and men who have grown critical of the unhealthy aspects of the competitive ethic are seeking to develop their sensitivity, openness, and expressiveness in order to strengthen the central area of their friendship networks.

Men need to change not only because it will enrich their lives, but because in the most literal way it can help them live longer. Men currently have a shorter life span than women: they smoke more and begin at an earlier age; their death rate from cancer is four times that of women; they suffer more heart attacks; they die of homicide four times as often as women, and commit suicide two and a half times more often. Male children also experience more developmental difficulties with speech and reading than female children.

It is perhaps conceivable that men are in some way genetically more vulnerable and fragile than women; but it seems far more likely that many of these problems stem from the social programming that men are subjected to. Male children are conditioned to be aggressive, daring, suspicious of both teammates and competitors, dominating of others. Such programming induces severe anxiety (which is the source of many health problems) and makes it difficult for men to engage in candid and mutually supportive relationships. It is no wonder that men have a great deal of trouble forming and maintaining close friendships. We have talked to many men who quite simply admit they have no real friends; and we've met many more who, wishing they had close friends, are actively taking positive steps to break down their traditional resistances to deeper friendship. Interestingly enough, we've found that the sympathetic understanding between close friends does indeed decrease the pressures and strains of their lives.

Many men's friendships begin in college, a time when people are particularly open to friendship because they are separated from family, home, and to a certain extent from the class or ethnic pressures of their upbringing. Jack and Rob formed what was to become a lifelong friendship when they discovered one evening that they shared a love of old movies, blues guitar, and cheap whiskey. They played and drank through the night, got sick and hung-over; but when they woke up and looked at each other and laughed, they knew they were going to be friends. They became inseparable buddies, hanging around with a crowd who shared their suspicions of the general corruption of society.

Jack and Rob's friendship was intensified by the disastrous consequences of their naïve attempt to provide some low-cost grass for their friends. They were arrested and discovered that they had been set up by the college authorities acting in concert with the local police. When arrested, each tried to protect the other by taking the blame. As Jack was brought into the police station, he found Rob sitting in handcuffs. "Gotta Camel, old buddy?" Rob asked wryly. Jack fumbled for a cigarette, placed it in Rob's mouth, and lighted it for him. Somehow this near-replay of one of their favorite movie scenes touched both of them deeply, and neither of them ever forgot it.

Their horrified parents bailed them out and hired prominent attorneys. They were able to have the charges reduced, and as a result, Rob and Jack were sentenced only to probation. Among other things, the probation provided that they avoid association with unsavory characters such as each other. Forced to leave school, they tentatively began exploring alternatives to the professional expectations their parents had had for them.

When Rob and Jack were able to resume their association, they discovered that they had moved in parallel directions. Their arrest had confirmed their conviction that a corrupt system would oppress people who rejected the dominant social norms. Jack found that what he really wanted to do with his life was to fight for social and political reform; he decided to become a freelance reporter and writer. Rob, for his part, chose to work as a counselor for disadvantaged children in inner-city schools. The bust, as Jack and Rob talked it over later, seemed to them the great test which had not only verified their loyalty and friendship but had also shown them how they really wanted to relate to the world.

Jack and Rob's friendship began when each was trying to figure out who he was and where he was going. Their confrontation with society only strengthened their friendship. But friends do not always have this kind of reaction to misfortune. Some fight, some flee, and some acquiesce.

Had Jack turned into a conformist "solid citizen" while Rob continued to rebel, their friendship would certainly have ended. Had they both capitulated, their mutual self-disgust would soon have split them apart.

Even close friendships like Jack and Rob's might have dissolved in post-college years due to geographical separation, marriage, career commitments, or differences in income. But their shared political outlook and sentiments have enabled their friendship to endure and have, in fact, brought them closer together.

Walt and Greg's friendship did not have to sustain attack from without, like Jack and Rob's, but it had to endure severe stresses from within, and it displayed astonishing strength when threatened. Walt and Greg had been buddies since going through officer training school together. Walt's wife, Thea, and Greg's wife, Barbara, felt almost as close as sisters. For some years the two families had shared barbecues, child-rearing problems, leaky roofs, and worn-out mufflers. However, their years of settled couple friendship came to an abrupt end one sunny Sunday over brunch when Thea revealed that she was having an affair. Walt was shocked and angry and, at first, self-righteous in his pain. Greg was pained by Walt's pain; and as they talked together about the situation in the ensuing weeks, Greg revealed that he too was worried about Barbara's increased interest in experimenting with sex with other men. The men's mutual distress about their wives, their discovery of the intensity of their own reactions, and a growing realization of their *own* unfulfilled needs and desires brought them much closer together. They found themselves talking on a more frank and intimate basis than they ever had before. Both remember this time as an arduous but productive period in which they were forced to confront problems that were difficult to handle; but in the end, that confrontation enriched their lives and relationship.

Greg and Thea were fairly close during this period, but their friendship remained platonic. Walt and Barbara, however, once ran into each other by chance in Los Angeles, at the house of a mutual friend. At the end of the evening, rather drunk, they went to Walt's motel and made love.

Thea learned of this brief encounter a year later and in her anger told Greg about it. He and Walt had a painful and ugly confrontation. Both remember this as the most agonizing moment of their lives. Greg recalls that he did not express his rage and feelings of betrayal—even though he suspected Walt really wanted him to, since it would have helped Walt expiate his own guilt and resolve his self-doubts about the kind of a friend he had been. The two men went through a long period of questioning the depth of their friendship, determining whether the rupture caused by the betrayal was irremediable, and searching for ways of coping with the disruption Thea's revelation had caused. Subsequently, both marriages broke up. Barbara and Thea found it impossible to resume their former easy and trusting contact, and they slowly drifted apart. The men, however, perhaps because their friendship went back so far, managed to "see enough of ourselves in each other," as Greg puts it, to understand and forgive. Indeed, their relationship at this point, they now recognize, somehow "clicked" in a new way. They had hit absolute bottom, and the friendship had survived and would become a lifelong commitment.

American men have traditionally related to each other through less personal concerns than did Walt and Greg.

Spectator sports, for instance, have given men an outlet for the emotional expression of their shared enthusiasm and solidarity; such sports have also provided opportunities for men to spend time together outside their couple relationships, watching events on TV or attending them together. Participant sports, on the other hand, have enabled men to form new bonds of comradeship, the results of shared vigorous activity, usually in all-male environments of gym or locker room. Participant sports have also allowed men to feel competitive within a framework of clearly and simply defined rules, unlike the world of work where perplexing moral issues often intervene.

Few Americans receive as much touching as the most "primitive" peoples gave one another. This lack is especially grievous for men, to whom any touch from another man may raise the unsettling question of homosexuality—in the other or in himself. At least in the dominant American WASP culture, men normally get to touch each other only in physical contact sports during their youth. The touching may be of the "crrrunch" variety, as in football, but our evolutionary mammalian constitutions are such that even rough or hostile touching is better than no touching at all. What warm physical contact most men receive comes from women and, for a few years, their children. Men occasionally can venture a pat on the back to show approval and affection for a fellow competitor who has done well. If sufficiently inebriated, they may drape an arm over the captive listener on the next barstool. But few men can unthinkingly put a hand on another man's arm or embrace another man upon greeting or leaving. They keep their distance, in the most literal sense.

Among young men in recent years there has been an interesting countermove to this: the "brotherhood handshake," a longer, fuller grasp of each other's hands from an angle that requires standing rather closer than the traditional handshake does. Originating in the counterculture of the sixties, it spread widely through the country, across class and cultural lines, though it seems to be used only among men. We believe that it symbolizes a broad and deeply felt male need for more intimate and meaningful ways of expressing their feelings and friendship to members of their own sex.

Men's traditional avoidance of the direct expression of emotion is not due to an inability to experience feelings deeply and relate emotionally to others; such abilities are inherent in all human beings. But the roles men are expected to play emphasize behaviors which exhibit a relatively narrow emotional range, compared to the emotional range expected of women. Men usually have a large vocabulary for understanding physical relationships; but they lack women's extensive emotional vocabulary, which enables them to recognize the subtleties in emotional relationships and thus choose from a wider range of emotional behaviors. Consequently, men often communicate their concern and loyalty for each other indirectly. Some men who would be willing literally to risk their lives for each other would never express their affection except through laconic, offhand remarks or joking behavior. Dean told us: "I have 'verbal friends'—they like to talk about everything, and we get into a lot of personal stuff. Then I have other friends who never talk about anything very private. But if I was in an emergency, they'd be the ones I'd turn to for help—and I'd get it."

As role flexibility in American society has increased, some men have begun to think critically about the traditional limitations on men's emotional lives and to feel uncomfortable with roles they see as constricting to themselves, their mates, and their friends. Feminists have pointed out the inequities in our society between the economic status of men and that of women; they have also emphasized what men have to gain in emotional options through women's liberation. Forced by the feminist movement to look closely at this, many men have discovered that they would enjoy being more expressive, more playful, more sensual, more open and exploratory where feelings are concerned, more communicative of "forbidden" emotions like fear, weakness, and uncertainty. Having acknowledged the pain and deprivation of not being able to express their feelings, such men realize that it is not only unfair but unhealthy for them to meet their need for emotional contact and sensitivity, compassion, and understanding almost totally through their relationships with women. They recognize that they must take equal responsibility for their friendships. Men who are beginning to achieve some degree of freedom in these areas tend to seek out others who share their aspirations. Through men's groups or other contacts, they are helping each other reassess their life patterns and relationships.

Once Peter's wife, Sylvia, became an active member of a feminist group, she began raising uncomfortable questions with Peter about their life. Why was she doing the housework and coping with the children? Why did he always feel under pressure to be the sole provider for the family? Why were there so many limitations on his emotional expression—his anger, affection, hopes, dreams? Peter realized that Sylvia's feminist activities had helped her to work through difficult issues and, when necessary, to confront him with demands for change in the way they lived. Many of her observations and conclusions struck him as painful but just, and these he could often accept with relative ease. At other times, however, the two of them would have bitter disagreements, make uneasy compromises, or come to painful stand-offs. The easiest issues concerned achieving an equitable division of housework and child care; Sylvia's wish to assume a work role that would be as satisfying and challenging to her as Peter's work was to him posed more difficult questions, since subtle changes in their relative self-concepts, their concepts of each other, and their psychological roles within the family would be involved.

Peter distinctly remembers feeling jealous of the support, sympathy, and understanding Sylvia received from her group. He wondered why men didn't form such mutual-support groups themselves—and he made up his mind to start one. He called his oldest and best friend, Ed, and a few other friends who he thought might be interested, either because they too were facing difficult situations at home or because they had shown a concern for emotional growth and self-development. He found it difficult to explain exactly what the group might do and fell back on saying: "You know, it'll be like a women's group, but for men. We need a place where we can meet regularly and feel safe to talk about our lives without pulling any punches."

Peter persuaded Ed and six other men he knew to join the group, and they met regularly each week, taking turns at each member's house. Gradually, they exposed their personal lives: Blake was on the verge of divorce; Mitchell had just gone through a traumatic breakup with several people he had lived with for years; Ted had ended a homosexual live-in arrangement and had begun a love affair with a woman; Simon, who had been married for ten years, was entering an "open" phase of marriage; and Jeremy was deeply worried about changing his career and lifestyle. In short, they were all confronting difficult issues on which they needed help, encouragement, and feedback. They also realized they needed an arena where they could discuss the implications of feminist ideas, which were increasingly important to all the women they were connected to: how men get locked into stereotyped behavior; how they treat women; how they feel about the ways women treat them; and how they could help each other learn better ways of relating, even if these involved painful readjustments of established living patterns. And they discovered that they could help each other express themselves more directly and emotionally. They gave each other permission to make mistakes, to be silly or weak on occasion, to feel and appear vulnerable.

Because competitiveness is one of the chief obstacles that men face in seeking to deepen friendships with each other, it became an issue that this group, like any men's group, had to deal with. In this group, a member busily self-criticizing his own chauvinist past might be brought up short with a comment: "Ah, stop having a more-sexually-screwed-up-than-thou attitude!" Another might delicately hint, in the way he talked about trying to escape the competitive rat race, that he had run it more successfully than anybody else in the room. There was even competition in adopting nurturing, sensitive behavior: Who could be the fastest learner of the new, gentler ways? Gradually, however, the group's conscious, constant monitoring and correction of such tendencies did "extinguish" at least some of the members' knee-jerk competitiveness; and the welcome by-product of this was a general lowering of anxiety and a subsequent opening-up of their most private selves.

Another issue that this group, like any men's group, had to confront was the sexual attraction men sometimes feel for one another, whether acted upon or not. The heterosexual members of this group were threatened, as some of them soon admitted, by Ted's bisexuality. They had fantasies that he might try to seduce them—and other fantasies that they might become attracted to him. Ted was sophisticated about such fantasies on the part of straight men, so he felt comfortable about bringing them into the open and dispatching them straightforwardly. Of course, nobody in the group fell for Ted, and he didn't fall for anybody either; friendship proved a more appealing relationship all around, especially after the others had learned from Ted that gay life posed much the same emotional and relationship problems as straight life. Gradually, the whole issue lost its edge. When the group began meeting in restaurants as well as homes, they even found that they could publicly express the warmth they felt for each other through hugs and pats without feeling constrained either by their own fears or concern about what other people might think.

Sometimes a friendship between two men lasts literally a lifetime and takes on a remarkable depth because of the many phases it has gone through. Roy and Gordon, who are now almost 40, met in the first grade and have considered each other their closest friend for most of the time since.

They played together at recess and sat together in class. Since their families were neighbors, they walked home together after school and played in the street and vacant lots of their small Eastern city. They look back on this period as one of tremendous intimacy, never really duplicated in adulthood. Their endless hours spent together were, as they remember them, an innocent yet complex and ever-shifting physical and largely nonverbal expression of their feelings for each other and the other members of their little "gang." It was friendship without reflection, doubt, or guilt. Yet Roy can now see that he was "into control and leadership"; Gordon says he was "into deferring." So they complemented each other without at that time giving any thought to the consequences; thirty years later, they were to realize how this pattern had afflicted them throughout their friendship.

By the seventh grade, Roy and Gordon regarded themselves as best friends. Yet, their interest in girls followed the same competitive pattern as their teenage sports activities, and their early sexual exploits were really meant to impress each other as well as other boys. They engaged in a great deal of typical male adolescent lying, pretense, and exaggeration about sex, with Roy usually having the best stories to tell.

Perhaps sensing a need to be on their own, away from each other as well as their families for a while, they went to different colleges. After graduation they shared a tiny apartment in New York. This period, however, was actually the most distant in their entire friendship. They were rarely home at the same time, and what they shared was mainly a feeling of being emotionally stalled.

In time, Roy moved to Los Angeles, began making money in plastics, and got married. Playing the instigator role as usual, he encouraged Gordon, increasingly restive over his father's expectations that he take over the family business, to join him. In the end, Gordon made the break. After a transitional period of guilt and depression at disappointing his father, during which Roy and his wife were his only real emotional contacts, he started a small business, and in time he too got married—to a friend of Roy's wife. The four fell into a two-couple friendship pattern, centered around family activities and their children. They spent weekends together at the beach or picnicked in the park, where Roy organized kite flying and Gordon conscientiously repaired the kites that crashed. It was a stable, "normal" period, with many homey satisfactions.

But looking back, the two men now think that they allowed their marital relationships to interfere with the development of better communication between themselves. This superficial and unreflective period ended mainly because their respective marriages broke up. Both men were deeply shaken, since each had come to identify himself above all as a good family man. Roy began meditation sessions in hopes of clarifying the possibilities for his future; Gordon also undertook a re-evaluation of his life. Since neither could confide in his wife any longer, they turned back to each other to discuss the painful issues they now faced. Gordon found that he welcomed this chance to be closer to Roy, and he realized that one issue he badly wanted to discuss was the leader-and-follower pattern of their friendship. After sharing his thoughts with Roy, Gordon was relieved and pleased that Roy too recognized that their old pattern of relating was an unhealthy and limiting one, and Roy gained added respect for Gordon in his newly found assertiveness in the relationship. In fact, their mutual perception of the ways their previous roles had interlocked became a special bond between them, and they took a wry pleasure ("Watch it—you're doing it again!") in catching each other if they occasionally fell back into their old routines.

Roy and Gordon's relationship became a mixture of mutual support and affectionate criticism, which suited them both. Having helped each other survive their marital difficulties and having put their own relationship on a dynamic and more equal basis, they feel their friendship will endure for life. They now follow each other's lives carefully and supportively: they know everything about each other's work, love lives, children. When one of them feels like discussing some problem, he calls up and arranges for "a little fix of friendship," which they jokingly regard as "cheaper than booze and much more effective." They can now talk to each other about literally anything, giving each other "full reports" without censoring anything or worrying about the effects of what they say. They

feel accepted and accepting, are proud of their friendship, and find that other friends admire them for it. It is,
at this point, the central focus of their lives.

Emotional closeness between men can develop in many
ways, sometimes planned but often not. Without consciously seeking to do so, a group of three businessmen
happened to develop an informal equivalent of a men's
group. Scott, who had an office in downtown Portland,
invited Leo and Elliot, whom he hadn't seen for several
years, to lunch at a small Italian café he had discovered.
Whether it was the easy, informal atmosphere of the restaurant, or the amount of wine that came with the lunch,
or something about their happiness at seeing each other
again, the three enjoyed some unusually personal conversation. Elliot recalls: "We all felt so good about it that we
agreed to meet again for lunch, at the same place the
following week. And that went well, too. We began to feel
like three members of a little club of our own. So we made
it a regular event."

Evidently there was something about this regular commitment of time to each other, with no "practical" end in
view or business to discuss, that made these lunches a
mechanism for the evolution of the men's friendships.
They soon found themselves discussing questions of emotional relationships and even business ethics which they
were unable to discuss in such an open way with anyone
else, even their wives. They were in different fields and
all doing equally well, so there was little direct competition among them, and each felt the others offered helpful
and disinterested advice. Gradually, they came to rely on
each other for counsel on a wide range of personal matters,
including their relations with wives and children, as well
as changes they wanted to make in their lives. Leo had
tired of suburban life and was trying to see how he could

return to the city yet retain some of the benefits of suburban living; Elliot was considering other career possibilities; and Scott was contemplating a separation from his wife. Over a period of several years, these men gave each other an unusual amount of understanding and support in confronting these difficult issues.

Occasionally, to provide some extra stimulation to their interaction, one of them would invite a fourth person to join them at lunch—someone who had something especially interesting going on in his life or who was knowledgeable in an area of mutual interest to the members of the group. But none of these guests became permanent members. Nor were women ever invited. Scott says: "I guess we all had women friends with whom we'd sometimes discuss the same sorts of things we talked about in the lunch group. But we must have all felt that a woman's presence might stir up a competitiveness that we had somehow managed to avoid feeling."

Though these three men had known each other before their lunches became a regular institution, and their friendships deepened markedly as a result of the "lunch club," they seldom saw each other socially; and if two of them happened to run into each other, their level of interaction was not as intimate as when all three were present. This may have been because the special chemistry of the group depended on the presence of all three, or perhaps because two of the men meeting separately felt a twinge of guilt at the absence of the third. In any event, when Elliot moved to another city, all three felt that their special friendship had suffered a fundamental change. Although Leo and Scott saw each other occasionally for a while, they now get together only when Elliot is in Portland, at which time the three make a point of returning to their old café and catching up on what has been happening in one another's lives.

These business friends were not, like Peter and his

friends, reacting to the concerns raised by the feminist movement. They simply enjoyed spending time with one another and discussing things they couldn't discuss with other men they knew. As Leo observes: "My suburban and office friends wanted to talk about cars or sports or crab grass. It all left me kind of high and dry." He remembers being relieved and delighted when he and Elliot and Scott moved into areas of feeling and emotion they had previously discussed only with women, and found that they could talk about them with men, too.

Through such exploration and experimentation, American men are discovering that they no longer need to short-change the emotional side of their nature. They are strengthening the central areas of their friendship networks and tapping new resources in each other to help meet emotional issues. In time, men and women will undoubtedly have learned enough from each other's strengths to have friendships and friendship networks that are not rigidly and traditionally male or female but flexibly and resourcefully human.

6.
Friendship in the Gay World

Gay people come from all socioeconomic classes, racial and ethnic backgrounds, religious and political persuasions, and geographic areas; and they are employed in virtually all fields. Yet, many gay people find it necessary to conceal their sexual preference because of potential conflicts with family, straight friends, community, or career.

In our major urban centers, where gay persons have been able to live more openly in recent years, it is apparent that homosexuality can be a total lifestyle and not merely an expression of sexual preference. Nonetheless, even in such communities gay people face considerable pressures which cause them to place special emphasis on friendship. Angela comes from a large, closely knit Italian-American family, with many strong emotional ties. During the formative stages of her adult life, Angela recalls, she attempted to reproduce the warmth and continuity of her family of origin by creating committed friendship relationships.

After college, Angela and several women friends, all heterosexual, moved from the Midwest to Seattle, where they rented a large, old house. They were soon joined by several men housemates. However, this living arrangement did not last long. The group decided to establish separate households: the women lived in one house, and the men rented a house around the corner. Some of the men and women became lovers within the overlapping friendship networks maintained by the two houses. They deliberately shared skills to break down sex-role stereotyping, making sure that everyone became competent in mechanical and domestic areas. They even held their money in a joint bank account, though this became problematic over time.

After several years, the women began to question why, if they were such close friends, and connected in so many ways, they didn't consider sleeping together. Feminist activities had brought them into contact with lesbian women who provided good models of lesbian relationships, and they explored the idea intellectually. They finally decided to "give it a try." The sexual experiment was fairly satisfying for the other two women, but for Angela it was initially a disaster. The intense emotional demands reminded her of past unwelcome sexual pressures from men; there was also the unexpected competition among the three women about who would sleep with whom, how often, and what it meant. When sexuality entered their friendship, Angela says, the situation immediately became more intense. Self-conscious discussions ensued as the women explored the distinctions between being friends and being lovers. For Angela, such discussions have continued over the years without the issues ever being resolved unambiguously or satisfactorily.

Through this period of change, relationships between the three women and their straight friends and lovers became increasingly strained; even so, the women's house still had the vision of building a family together and remaining committed "forever, beyond the pleasure or displeasure of the moment." The women's house was never separatist, but the practical difficulties of integrating the two households slowly became insuperable.

In time, Angela's housemates "came out" and attacked Angela for not doing the same. Even when Angela did, the feelings of estrangement did not ease; in fact, they became more and more intense. Finally, her housemates acknowledged that they were a committed couple and moved into a small apartment together. Meanwhile, Angela fell in love with another woman; and although she is quite happy in this new relationship, she is aware that she and her lover can never be long-term friends in the same way her former housemates are. She reflects: "If we three, who loved one another so much, couldn't make it, even being dedicated radicals and feminists, who can?"

Not only was the break with her old friends painful to her, but she found that people they knew tended to take sides. This created an especially difficult situation, for in the small gay community where they all lived, people were constantly running into each other. A little sadly, Angela wonders whether her positive early family experiences gave her unreasonably high expectations for friendships. She and her lover now live in a five-person household where they continue to seek stability and warmth from a family-type network of friends, which includes both straight and gay men and women, among them Angela's two old friends.

Another gay woman, Christy, feels the attempt to make family out of friends is more characteristic of gay women than straight women because gays are more cut off from ordinary sources of family support and stability. Straight people tend to structure their lives around long-term commitments to children and interconnections with schools, churches, and neighborhoods. Gay people with children also participate to some extent in such networks, but some gays without children feel a special need to provide long-term structure for their lives through safe, committed gay friendships. Also, some gay people, knowing they will not continue their family lines, fear a generational discontinuity that can be somewhat assuaged by cultivating friendship networks over the years or by establishing godparent or other supportive relationships with their friends' children.

Gay women have access to somewhat different social resources, and thus have different friendship potentials open to them, than do gay men. As Harriet found when she came to San Francisco, there are relatively few gay women's events or political groups that can serve as meeting places. There are also fewer gay women's bars than men's bars, which tend to transcend class and style barriers. Harriet joined the softball team for a gay bar and found that activities of that sort cut across class differences quite effectively. Harriet is a professional person but lives with a woman of working-class origins, and many of their gay friends work in trades such as printing, electrical installation, and house renovation.

Racism, on the other hand, is an issue that Harriet feels the gay community has not dealt with very effectively. Although she has straight black and Latina colleagues at work, she lives a racially segregated private life, which she regrets. There are many black and Third World lesbians in the area, but lifestyle differences tend to keep them separate. Latina and Asian lesbians often are still subject to intense pressure from their families and prefer to live a closet existence. Harriet believes there is more contact among people of different racial backgrounds in the gay world than in straight society, but she nonetheless feels there is still racism in the gay community, which hinders interracial friendships.

In the gay world as in the straight world, social attitudes tend to determine sexual behavior as much as sexual behavior influences social attitudes. For someone living as a closet homosexual, lifestyle and friendship patterns are sharply separated from sexual activity. However, for someone who has come out and made a positive commitment to the gay lifestyle, sexual choices usually become integrated into the subculture's settled pattern of living, in which emotional problems of personal relating take on the same complexity and difficulty they have for heterosexuals. To these are added, of course, the problems of discrimination—the threat of job loss, arrest, blackmail, and extortion. Such problems make it necessary for many gay people to develop acute social perceptions and abilities for role playing and sometimes protective dissembling. Lesbians are especially subject to economic discrimination and are thus even more likely than gay men to compartmentalize their lives, keeping their sexuality separate from their work or public lives.

As Margaret Mead has observed, there is a well-documented, normal human capacity to love members of both sexes. Probably a majority of people are bisexual in this sense, and substantial numbers experiment with their own sex at some time in their lives. But the basic sexual choices people make are a consequence of the way they have been brought up—specifically, to select partners within a fixed group. For our society this pattern has been heterosexual, with a homosexual alternate culture hidden within it. It is conceivable, as Mead implies, that a future society might offer its members a free choice of sexual activity, thus opening up a great complexity of possibilities to be explored. Some people go through phases of interest in and attraction to mainly one sex; others, finding it difficult to be completely fulfilled by either one sex or the other, maintain simultaneous or alternate sexual contacts with people from both sexes. People may also prefer the social satisfactions and friendship modes of the gay or straight worlds quite apart from their sexual preferences.

Virginia, a bisexual, has sometimes found that although she basically prefers sex with women, she has fallen in love with and has had good sexual experiences with men. But bisexuality today is usually a transitional stage or a peripheral activity. Although there are bisexuals who sleep only with other bisexuals, there is as yet no such thing as an established bisexual subculture or lifestyle with which they can identify. A person who has entered a steady sexual relationship has by that fact chosen either a gay or straight lifestyle; by selecting a regular gay sexual partner, a person also selects a gay support group and mainly gay friends, becomes sensitized to gay issues, and usually creates a distance with the family of origin.

Members of the gay community tend to feel that bisexuality is a wishful fiction, though this is not necessarily because they are opposed to heterosexual contacts. Lucille, who has lived as a lesbian for eight years, points out that the cost of being in love with a person of your own sex is extremely high and defines almost everything else in your life. Casual affairs are of little personal and social cost and can, of course, be with people of either sex, she says; but when a primary commitment is involved, it must be either gay or straight. Lucille, acknowledging that she may be stereotyping here, maintains that bisexuality is easier and more overt for gay men because sex for them is somewhat more independent of relationships. She adds that for straight women, whose principal emotional support comes from their spouse, an occasional bisexual experience with a woman is merely peripheral.

Lucille also notes an interesting aspect of friendships among gay women, and between gay and straight women. Because gay women have greater experience of and information about the emotional and sexual possibilities of women's relationships, they must consciously choose their level of intensity and intimacy in a friendship. Usually this means a self-conscious holding back from the kind of interaction that could become sexual, which parallels what heterosexual men and women experience. Lucille has found such limiting easiest when each of the women is involved in a stable couple commitment.

Both homosexual and bisexual people are often seen as threatening by heterosexuals, and these feelings can prevent new friendships from forming and destroy or limit old ones. Coming out thus usually entails a wholesale rearrangement of friendship patterns, as does the process of a gay person "going straight." Lucille remarks that revealing your homosexuality or bisexuality to good heterosexual friends makes them wonder about their own potentialities in those directions—potentialities they often would rather not have to think about. Homosexuals sometimes find bisexuals threatening in a similar way.

Straight parents, though they might be prepared to accept gays as friends, are often disturbed if they come into contact with parents who are openly gay. Yet gay parents are numerous. More than 50 percent of all gay people have experienced earlier heterosexual relationships. About 20 percent of gay people have been married, and about the same number have had children. There are an estimated one million lesbian mothers in the United States, most of them rearing children from former marriages, and a few adopting children and rearing them with their lovers. Legal difficulties for gay parents are gradually being overcome; in fact, gay men are in some cases being allowed to adopt children or are being granted custody of them after a divorce.

It is as yet totally unknown what effects, if any, such upbringing will have on children's lives; it does, of course, produce social problems for them, but apparently in communities like San Francisco and New York these are not insurmountable. Camilla, the 12-year-old daughter of a lesbian mother openly but discreetly living with her gay lover, admits that while it's hard for some people to accept her living situation at first, they usually come around in time. It's not too difficult for her, she says; after all, almost half of her age-mates live in single-parent or blended families, and everybody has to make adjustments. Even so, straights, though they realize that most homosexuals grew up with heterosexual parents, often fear the influence of adult gays on children. Camilla's mother had moved to a residential neighborhood with many children and good facilities for them. Yet one of Camilla's friends was forbidden by her parents to play at Camilla's house, though the mothers maintained a façade of cordiality.

In many cities there is a complex intermingling of the gay and straight worlds. Gerald, a gay man who is "not sexually adventurous," as he puts it, lives in a settled, monogamous relationship with his lover. When Gerald moved in with his lover, he encountered a problem typical of straight marriages: his lover became very possessive and resented the time Gerald spent not only with his former lovers but with his straight friends, even straight women friends. His friendships have become somewhat subsidiary, as is common with all couples, but Gerald continues to keep them up, regarding this as a deliberate maintenance of a support network, a necessary defense against the discrimination and hostility to which gay people are subjected.

One of Gerald's important friendships was with Maxine, a straight woman he had met while he was still straight, through a friendship with her husband. They became very close; and when she and her husband divorced, Gerald found himself, rather painfully and reluctantly, on Maxine's side. By this time, he had begun to have mostly homosexual relationships; but because Maxine badly needed support from friends, he felt that an affair with him might help her. Maxine, however, was not interested in extending their relationship in that direction. Gerald then attempted to integrate her into his gay circle; but that was complicated by her affair with a man who felt uncomfortable around gays and by the unenthusiastic reaction of Gerald's lover, who perceived Maxine as a rival for Gerald's attention. About this time, Gerald and his lover moved to a distant part of the city, and his relationship with Maxine ended, to their mutual regret. Gerald hopes that as time goes by, the barriers to friendship between straight and gay people will gradually erode.

Diana is a heterosexual physician with a wide range of friends. Her best woman friend, Carey, is a professor, also in her mid-thirties and heterosexual, who for many years has lived next door and shared a common circle of friends. Diana's best man friend, Dennis, is a gay artist. When he first came to Los Angeles, eight years ago, the two women "adopted" him into their social circle. Diana remembers that the connection she made with Dennis was immediate and had none of the usual tentativeness of new friendships; she attributes this to the fact that her father had just died, as had Dennis's mother. Because Diana and Dennis were in an open state of grief, they quickly empathized with each other's pain.

Dennis moved into an apartment in the neighborhood where Diana and Carey lived. Diana and Dennis went out together socially but did not indulge in the charade of being a heterosexual couple, which some gay people use for protective coloration. This was particularly risky for Diana, who has learned that going out with a gay person makes you vulnerable to the possibility that straight people will assume you too are gay. However, Diana's relatives liked and accepted Dennis, and he and Diana were often invited to family dinners. Both enjoyed the comfortable feeling that resulted from being part of a stable social group.

While Diana and Dennis initially acknowledged a certain attraction between them, Diana thought that any sexual involvement would probably destroy their relationship; moreover, Dennis was mainly interested in men, particularly the gay cruising scene. As it turned out, their refraining from having sex became a major bond between them. Many heterosexuals believe that the opportunity for a good heterosexual liaison will somehow reclaim a homosexual person for "normal" life. This is a fantasy, far removed from the realities of gay life. Diana, however, never had any thoughts of "saving Dennis for heterosexuality" and accepted his need to come to terms with being gay.

Often, Diana and Dennis disagreed sharply—about art, music, literature—but they learned that they could oppose or even tease each other in a nonthreatening way. Gradually, they grew to depend on each other's fairness and good sense, and a fierce loyalty developed on both sides. They also reserved the right to disapprove of each other's sexual partners and other friends, sometimes scathingly. Yet, though both of them were quite jealous and possessive in their love affairs, they never suffered such feelings in their friendship. Dennis particularly respected Diana's friendship with Carey, to whom he had also become close, and accepted the role of Diana's peripheral friends in her life, even when he didn't especially like them. Although Diana disapproved of the promiscuity of

Dennis's sex life, she realized that it was one of the reasons why their friendship was so important to him. The solid foundation of their relating countered the feelings of loneliness and vulnerability that can arise from a sexual life of transient encounters—feelings also experienced by heterosexuals whose sex lives are relatively fluid.

If friendships such as Diana and Dennis's seem unusual to many straight people, it is even harder for them to understand gay housemate arrangements. Shelby, a gay woman who lives in the same household as a gay man, points out that opposite-sex gay housemates can be close platonic friends. The fact is that many gay men who have gay women housemates have never slept with a woman. As one such man told us: "The thought has never entered my mind." And the same holds true for many gay women. Indeed, the emotional security of living intimately with a person you are not tempted by sexually is one of the chief advantages of gay house-sharing, since it allows you to enjoy the social variety of living with persons of the opposite sex without the complications often posed by having opposite-sex heterosexual housemates. Yet, many young heterosexual people now living together casually and easily in mixed-sex households are also reaping the benefits of nonsexual friendships.

While research on the homosexual population is still in its early stages, in general the emotional problems of gay interpersonal relationships, whether in love or friendship, appear to parallel those of heterosexuals. Gay people often live substantial parts of their lives within the bounds of the gay subculture, which has to some extent its own manners and habits, but the fact of having different sexual

preferences in itself does not mean a fundamental difference in people's lives or friendship patterns. Some survey
findings indicate that gay men tend to have more close
friendships, mainly but not exclusively with other gays,
than do straight men. It has also been well documented
that gay relationships span a range—from stable, long-
term monogamous commitments to temporary, physical
liaisons—comparable to the range found in heterosexual
relationships.

As Don, who has lived in the gay world for five years,
observes, gay usage of the term "friend" is not exactly the
same as that of the straight world. It may mean "nonsexual acquaintance," including a straight acquaintance;
at the other end of the spectrum, it may mean "current
steady sexual partner," implying a relationship less serious
and less intimate than that of "lover"; and there is a series
of intermediate meanings, indicated by social context,
intonation, and body language. These subtle usages parallel those of the straight world, where the terms "boy-
friend" and "girlfriend" are now widely seen as demeaning
and sexist, "lover" has become too old-fashioned, and
"woman-friend" and "man-friend" are not yet generally
accepted alternatives.

Don emphasizes that many gay people's best friends are
not gay and that friendships flourish across sexual-prefer-
ence lines just as they do across the barriers of gender and
age. Don's best friend is a straight man, and there is nothing sexual in the relationship. Their basic bond, Don says,
is intellectual: they both have playfully exploratory minds
and share literary tastes, which gives them numerous
opportunities for lengthy, intricate discussions. They are
members of a literary social circle of writers, professors,
and publishers, which includes men and women, some
gay, some straight.

Don reports that most of his gay friendships originated

in specifically sexual contexts, though other gay people have told us of friendships that grew out of shared interests or common situations that had nothing to do with sex. Don looks back on his two main gay friendships as having started as "lust." After a time, as Don sees it, such initial physical attractions have to go in one of two directions: either they develop into love and a total emotional commitment, or the sexual side wanes and friendship may or may not develop.

Although Don, like many gay people, sought an ideal sexual partner who would also be a very close friend, neither of the two lovers who subsequently became his nonsexual friends fulfilled this ideal. He attributes this to the fact that both were somewhat older and thus, perhaps, filling his need for a guide or mentor—or even father—in the gay world of which he had only recently admitted he was a member.

Sex, to Don, is a kind of universal language in the gay community, a way of making contact. Sexual release is by no means always its main purpose. Many of Don's gay friends who enjoy sex for "purely aesthetic reasons" regard it as a game to be played at the highest levels of sensitivity, imagination, and freedom. Just as in the straight world where an initial romantic seduction may be followed by a transition to a warm and loving relationship, so in the gay world stylish sensual encounters may in time develop into relationships with deep emotional components.

7.

Sex and Friendship

Every male-female friendship has sexual components, whether acknowledged or not. Some people prefer to deny sexual feelings because they raise issues that are threatening and troublesome for them; others recognize that these feelings can enrich the relationship, though they may decide not to express them explicitly; and still others feel that they should express and enjoy their sexual feelings with their friends. What is important is that you recognize your right to handle the sexual elements in friendship in whatever way is most comfortable for you and to maintain clarity about what you and your friends feel is satisfying and appropriate in the friendship at any given point.

Vicki is one of the many people who refuse to give sexual considerations any importance in friendship. Happily married and monogamous, Vicki does not allow herself to imagine that a friendship with a man might become sexual. "An affair is just not in my game plan," she says. "If a man begins to get the wrong idea, I make sure he knows what my feelings and intentions are. I've found most men are pleased to have the air cleared—in fact, some of them are downright relieved not to have to come on sexually. A lot of men I know have so much trouble with sexual relationships these days that a simple friendship sounds much more appealing to them than something sexual and complicated." Vicki considers herself a clear-minded, firm person, and she doesn't understand how other people can have so much trouble where sex and friendship are concerned. She is obviously very fond of one of her long-standing male friends but exclaims: "If he ever laid a hand on me, I'd break his arm!"

Valerie is 18 and thus a member of a supposedly more sexually "free" generation; nonetheless, she has arrived at a position rather similar to Vicki's. She has tried to maintain nonsexual friendships with young men but finds that sooner or later they begin to pressure her sexually. "I thought we had gotten to a point where men as well as women were sophisticated enough to respect each other's feelings about sex—not just adopt stereotyped sex roles. But the men I meet still feel they've got to be sexually aggressive, as if women always expect them to come on." Valerie has become so embittered by her experiences that she has virtually abandoned any attempt to establish friendships with men.

The difficulties of handling sexual issues in friendships have led some people to have only same-sex friends. Janet, in her early life, had perceived women only as friends and men only as sexual partners. She was also convinced that men were incapable of simple friendships with women and would always push in a sexual direction. She later observed, however, that her women friends often had male friends who were not lovers or even former lovers. Consequently, Janet decided to explore the possibilities for herself. She began to cultivate her acquaintance with Josh, a happily married man, who was a fellow member of the geology department in a large construction company. Josh's intelligence, empathy, and spirit of cooperation made him an easy and comfortable person to be around; in fact, the way they worked together somehow reminded her of her friendships with women.

One day after they had made a joint presentation of

some research findings to a government agency, Janet suggested they have lunch together. At the outset, she was rather nervous. She knew they were both exhausted from the presentation and had no desire to discuss it, yet she didn't know what else they could talk about. To her relief, Josh began telling her how anxious he had been about the presentation and recounted some funny stories about similar experiences he had had in the company. They soon found themselves chatting easily about people they worked with and discovered they even had some mutual acquaintances outside the office. At the end of the meal, Janet noted that Josh had made no attempt to introduce any sexual elements into the conversation. She felt, in fact, that the lunch had been just as satisfying and unproblematic as a lunch with a woman who might become a friend. The experience was most encouraging, and her relationship with Josh gradually developed into a friendship. After some months, she realized that she had crossed her formerly self-imposed barriers when she found herself comfortably discussing with Josh a sexual relationship she was having with a man, just as she might have discussed it with a woman.

Sometimes the tendency to have only same-sex friends is not due so much to discomfort with the sexual possibilities of opposite-sex friendships as to the different quality of feeling endemic to same-sex friendships. Josephine is not alarmed by the sexual aspect of friendships with men but does prefer friendships with women because she feels there's more intuitive understanding, more openness with them. "And I always sense some kind of tension in a friendship with a man. I find myself watching my step. It's just not easygoing."

A pattern of having only same-sex friends is, we believe, a serious limitation of our friendship potential; there are aspects of the human condition which we can truly appreciate only by understanding the opposite sex. People who find themselves avoiding opposite-sex friendships should consider whether they are doing so because of unresolved or conflicted feelings. For example, it is fairly common for men to have deep unconscious fears of women. Consequently, they feel able to deal with women only in the safely defined context of a sexual relationship, in which they perceive themselves as dominant, and unable to tolerate the equal relationship that friendship demands.

There are also people who have only opposite-sex friends. Some men seem unable to form friendships with other men, either because of intense competitiveness, lack of available models, or fear of homosexuality. Some women devalue all relationships with other women, concentrating their attention—erotic or otherwise—on men.

Sheldon, who prizes opposite-sex friendships, summarizes what many people see as their main attraction: "You can enjoy being with a member of the opposite sex without the enormous burden of expectations we put on sexual partnerships." We would add that such friendships also avoid the effects of the projective and defensive mechanisms which a sexual relationship entails. Thus, compared to most sexual relationships, opposite-sex friendships are refreshingly realistic and frank.

Sometimes people who have shared a nonsexual friendship decide to make love. This can have both negative and positive repercussions. Miriam had a long-term friendship with a man she had known while she was married. After her divorce, their lives intersected at work and socially, and they saw each other fairly often. They had a certain playful, sexual attraction for each other and teased about someday going to bed together. Although they occasionally fooled around a little, something would always happen to prevent them from making love. After some years of this, they finally slept together. But it didn't work. The sex was okay but nothing special; yet it changed something in their relationship—the magic edge was gone— and they both regretted it. It took them several years to "obliterate" the "mistake," which they accomplished by scrupulously avoiding any reference to it, as if it were a secret they had to conceal. By depriving the episode of any connection with their ongoing relationship, they managed to erase it from their personal history and were finally able to return to the comfortably playful relationship they had once had.

People who seek to defuse rising sexual feelings should probably begin with a frank acknowledgment of them; avoiding the situation will not help and may even intensify sexual desires. The acknowledgment of attraction, however, must be accompanied by a firm statement of the intention not to act on it. Thinking back, Miriam realizes that she had enjoyed the mild degree of flirtation with her friend more than she had enjoyed sleeping with him. She wishes she had committed herself to their not becoming lovers; such restraint, she feels, can constitute a shared achievement that both friends can be proud of and respect. There are other people who, in Miriam's situation, might try nonsexual bodily contact—discreet hugs, walking arm-in-arm—which can provide some of the physical touching they desire but have usually experienced only through sex.

An increasing number of people take the view that sexuality is a natural and delicious part of any opposite-sex friendship and that it should be neither discounted nor avoided. For them, it is a potentially enriching aspect of friendship. Eloise has often had satisfying friendships that included sex. She says: "We're lucky enough to be living in a time that gives you a lot of new opportunities. People no longer feel that any friendship between a man and a woman inevitably leads to sex. The paradox is, now that we know it *doesn't* always happen, we can relax about it if it does. Sex with friends is like other shared pleasures. You can enjoy it if you both feel like it, but it isn't the big deal it used to be."

As social and economic equality of men and women has grown, members of both sexes have come to have similar lifestyles and thus similar views and experiences. Now that we live with somewhat different sexual attitudes, women expect to exercise their right to be as interested in sex and as sexually active as men; the sexual aspect of relationships is thus becoming egalitarian. Men and women can both matter-of-factly acknowledge that they enjoy sex; and if they engage in it, it is an equal and open exchange. Eloise has been friends with Ben for two years. Both are marathon runners, and it is their shared passion for running which is their real friendship bond. They both have regular lovers to whom they are deeply attached. But, Eloise speculates, if she and Ben happened to be at the other end of the country for a marathon and happened to be feeling sexy at the same time, they'd probably make love. She is sure, however, that it would be nothing more than a detail in the mosaic of their friendship.

People who mix sex and friendship don't assume they will sleep with every friend to whom they happen to be attracted—part of the vital spark of such friendships is that years might pass before anything sexual happens, if it ever does. Yet, just acknowledging the possibility seems liberating and invigorating. "If there *isn't* anything sexual in a friendship with a man," Joyce told us, "I know that friendship doesn't have much of a future. After you've built up a certain trust and intimacy, it seems artificial to me not to express this warmth sexually." Joyce also says that curiosity is a strong motive for her, especially with relatively nonverbal friends. She feels that knowing such persons sexually has given her insights into their character she could never have obtained otherwise.

Joyce feels relatively comfortable when a friendship becomes sexual and then goes back to being nonsexual. "What's crucial," she says, "is to keep it absolutely clear between the two people involved what is going on at any given moment. Of course, if I'm interested in letting it get sexual and my friend doesn't want to, we have a problem. You both have to pay attention if the other person's upset, and you both have to work at not allowing that to jeopardize the friendship."

Louise, a traveling sales representative, lives with a man in her hometown. Because Louise is on the road so much, they have agreed that they may each sleep with other people so long as doing so does not threaten their own relationship or cause the other embarrassment.

Louise has several men friends scattered throughout her territory whom she regularly contacts when she is in town; some are single, some are married. She never knows for sure what will happen sexually, but she knows there will be good talk of old times, probably a pleasant lunch or dinner, and occasionally she will find herself in bed with one of them. Louise is extremely fond of all of them —perhaps, she says wryly, because she sees them only twice a year. She notes that these sexual friendships have lasted longer than any romantic relationship she has ever had with men in her own city. Although she hopes someday to settle down permanently with a man, she frankly admits that she would never consider giving up her friends in other cities. "It's hard to hold your life together when you travel," she says, "and these men give me a sense of continuity. They're the emotional landmarks on the map of my territory." Louise clearly feels that her ability to combine enduring friendship and intermittent sex is one of the keys to her successful life adjustment.

Annette works in the media and divides her time between New York, where she lives with her stockbroker-husband, and Washington, where she often spends several consecutive days on business. Annette and her husband are in their late forties, get along well, and have a good life together. Annette maintains that it is possible to combine sex with friendships outside a marriage so long as such relationships remain low-key and are hidden from the spouse. Annette distinguishes between clandestine affairs with mutual friends or business associates—which she finds sordid, especially if the lovers live in the same locality—and casual or intermittent sex with people safely outside the couple's social and professional orbits. Annette is not entirely comfortable with concealment of such relationships from her husband, but she is willing to accept this discomfort because she has observed that people who attempt to be totally candid about attractions to others may often destroy their marriage.

When Annette is in Washington, she often spends time with Terry, an artist and teacher whom she met five years ago at the Smithsonian Institution and with whom she has had a sexual relationship. Terry, an attractive man, is usually surrounded by women; and at the time he met Annette, he had no need for another lover. However, he found Annette's rather cynical wittiness appealing, and it was refreshing for him to spend time with a dynamic and energetic person who was not involved in the art world in any way. In addition, as a journalist, she had a quick understanding of the politics of the art world, and she helped him laugh at it and gain a perspective on the games art people play. They discovered that they could usefully criticize each other's work—perhaps because both were operating outside their normal power connections but from positions of mutual trust.

Terry and Annette saw each other on Annette's expeditions to Washington; and after several months, their friendship had clearly become important to both of them. Annette believes that unless she had taken the initiative, the friendship might have remained nonsexual. However, one assignment required her to be in Washington for ten days, during which time she realized that she was sexually attracted to Terry. She was uneasy about revealing this, but once she finally did, Terry grinned and said: "Well, I'm glad you brought it up. I've been having some sexy thoughts about you, too!" Annette remembers wondering whether she was obliged to make it absolutely clear to Terry that she was not interested in having some kind of overwhelming affair with him and so was relieved when Terry said: "Let's do it, but no promises, no obligations!" They went to bed, and Annette was surprised at the intensity and satisfaction of the sex they had together. Until then, she had rather assumed that good sex was possible only with people you deeply loved, and she certainly didn't love Terry. But somehow being in bed with him was such good fun: it was as if the absence of romance allowed her to simply be herself, something she had never quite been able to do with other casual lovers.

She assumed events would follow the same pattern when she returned to Washington some weeks later. But Terry was involved in a new affair with one of his models; and although he wanted to see Annette, his sexual energy was focused in a different direction. Initially taken aback by Terry's attitude, Annette soon realized that the uncertainty about whether or when she and Terry would go to bed again had an unanticipated positive aspect to it. Since theirs was a relationship "without expectations," she found that when sexual things did happen they were doubly exciting. Her experiences with Terry were powerful, but because the relationship was fundamentally a friendship, she never felt it threatened her commitment to her marriage.

Sex can be used as a dramatic gesture within a friendship as a means of clarifying or resolving a difficult situation. Tim and Craig were old college chums who had been close for seven or eight years. After college, Tim became involved with Dorothy. The two were not only lovers but also extremely good friends, and they eventually married. After a year or so, they realized that their initial unconsidered assumption of monogamy did not really suit them, so they decided to allow themselves to be open to sexual relationships with others, even if this experimentation might create pain and difficulty.

Although Dorothy had become close with many of Tim's friends, her relationship with Craig remained uneasy. The intimacy between Tim and Craig somehow seemed threatening to her, and the deepening of Tim's relationship with her made Craig feel increasingly left out. Tim was well aware of the situation.

One night Craig slept over in the tiny studio apartment where Dorothy and Tim were living. He laid his sleeping bag on a mat in the corner of the room and climbed in. Dorothy and Tim, having snuggled with each other for a half-hour, waiting for Craig to go to sleep, began to make love. They were as quiet as they could be, but Craig's restless turnings this way and that made it plain he was still awake.

After a time, Dorothy, impelled by what she later called "a kind of instinct," slipped out of bed, went over to Craig's corner, crept into his sleeping bag, and made love with him. In the morning, though they never discussed the matter, it was clear that they all felt that some kind of barrier had been broken. In some symbolic way, Craig would no longer feel excluded from an important aspect of Tim's life; Dorothy felt closer to Craig and no longer threatened by his friendship with Tim; and Tim was impressed by Dorothy's spirited, unexpected action and pleased that the three of them had achieved another level of intimacy.

Such bold adventures in mixing sex and friendship are not for everyone. But whatever adjustments to the combination of sex and friendship people make in their lives, the one essential factor is clarity. For many years, Ingrid had sex with her men friends but remained confused about what she was after. Abstractly, she thought that if friend- ship with a man was a good thing, wouldn't it be even better if they occasionally made love? But for Ingrid it didn't work that simply. When she had sex with a friend and it went well, she began to yearn for more and to hope that the relationship would develop into something more serious. Although Ingrid has never married, she sees herself as actively looking for a husband. Evidently her intense desire for a permanent love relationship makes her quick to grasp at the possibility of a friendship turning into one once it has become sexual. "Instead of looking for men who are really husband material," she says, "I keep trying to turn friends into husbands." This, of course, makes it impossible for her to continue being "just friends" with a man she has slept with. She becomes jealous of his attentions to or sexual relations with other women; and inevitably the relationship comes to a crisis which may, she has found to her distress, end up by destroying the friendship.

Reuben suffers a different kind of confusion. He is normally attracted to women with whom he could never be friends, and women who strike him as potential friends are somehow never appealing sexually. Reuben has women friends who he knows are very attractive, but they do not turn him on. Several of these friends have indicated that they would be interested in sleeping with him. Reuben feels that he needs to deal with his sexual preoccupation with women who would never make satisfactory partners in a serious love relationship or marriage, so he has gone to bed with these friends on occasion. The experiences, however, have not helped Reuben overcome his problem, and he has entered psychotherapy in hopes of discovering the roots of his dilemma.

Some married couples who wish to remain open to sexual friendships realize that such relationships may not remain low-key—in the manner of Annette's friendship with Terry—and that they may develop into full-blown affairs, with destructive consequences for the partnerships. A novel attempt to maintain clarity and minimize such possibilities was made by Margo and Ken, who restricted their sexual friendships to their common circle of friends and made sure that what went on was openly discussed at all times. They maintain that if you're going to have sexual friendships, you might stay married longer if you have them with people whom everybody knows. Margo and Ken feel that romance and infatuation of the kind that can occur with relative strangers—even *without* sex being involved—is a far greater menace to marriage than relatively casual sex with friends you know too well to fall for.

The objective, as Margo and Ken see it, is to provide themselves with variety, adventure, and the chance for warm, friendly experiences of intense relating. But they want their adventures to be nonthreatening and noncompetitive, without the fear of possibly losing the mate. Their ideal, in a way, is an integrated, satisfied, extended "happy family." They contrast this frank and open approach with the traditional practice of having clandestine affairs, which have the potential for discovery, feelings of betrayal and anguish, and subsequent distrust.

"After all," Ken contends, "sleeping with a friend is really no different from putting a large amount of energy into a work project with that friend or spending a lot of time helping a friend through some crisis." If this perspective on sexual friendships can be maintained, such arrangements as Ken and Margo's can work for a time. Sooner or later, however, one of the sexual friendships is likely to develop into a serious affair that threatens someone intolerably, and the whole system will become unstable. For it to work in the first place, each mate must feel equally satisfied with his or her extramarital partner. While intensity of sexual experience enters into this, it is by no means the only or even dominant factor; what people are really concerned about is how they are being treated in comparison to their mate's lover. Thus, a great deal of emotional stability is required to withstand the inevitable stress.

One way Ken and Margo try to keep anxieties under control is for each to have a veto power over any sexual involvement the other might undertake. This, and the ability to discuss frankly what is going on, provides safety valves for the painful feelings of insecurity, loss of intimacy, and resentment that inevitably build up.

Such precautions, however, suffice only if everyone involved operates on the basis of honesty and good will— which most people cannot sustain. Therapists who have worked with people attempting this kind of experiment report that it frequently endures up to six months on a more or less successful basis but that it rarely lasts more than a few years. Most couples who try it finally make a conscious decision to abandon it because the strains and difficulties involved are simply not worth the satisfaction gained.

From the viewpoint of a friend having a sexual relationship with one partner in a marriage, the arrangement can be fulfilling for a time. Barry was part of the family circle of Naomi and Phillip, a couple who ran a very open house and had a party every weekend. Their house was always crowded with guests, and the cellar was full of gallon jugs of wine they bought from a friend's vineyard. Even though both Phillip and Naomi had a number of sexual friendships, they loved each other deeply, had three children to whom they were devoted, and intended to stay together. Their objective in their unorthodox social and sexual life was to live adventurously with style but to preserve stability and continuity.

Barry admired Phillip and Naomi's relationship and their skill in combining their sexual and social lives. He was also pleased that Naomi found him interesting and attractive. One evening when Barry gave a big party of his own, Phillip left early; and after the party was over, Barry and Naomi made love. Over the next few days, Naomi and Phillip talked things over and agreed that Barry had no desire to threaten their marriage. When they told Barry of this conversation, he confirmed that he prized their friendship too much to jeopardize it by allowing his relationship with Naomi to get out of hand. On this basis, the relationship flourished. Barry spent even more time at Naomi and Phillip's house, and Phillip and the children accepted him as a constant in their lives. Once, when Phillip was away and Barry slept over with Naomi, the children came in early and found them in bed. "Oh," one of them piped up, "Barry's playing Daddy!" This seemed to cause the children no confusion, perhaps because they sensed the firm rules within which this "play" went on.

The arrangement suited all the parties quite well for about a year. But then Barry began to feel the need to find a woman with whom he could have a deeper, more committed relationship—a woman free to live with him and perhaps marry him. He knew that even if he wanted to he could never replace Phillip in Naomi's life. In time, Barry concluded that his sexual friendship with Naomi was preventing him from putting his energy into a serious love affair with someone else; and so long as he remained a subordinate member of their circle, he was not altogether in charge of his own life. He therefore stopped sleeping with Naomi, who sadly accepted his motives for doing so, and thenceforth saw much less of her and Phillip. But he still remembers the time he spent with them as one of the most interesting periods of his life.

New living arrangements are gradually breaking down separations between men and women, and this tends to demystify the other sex. When members of the opposite sex are seen more realistically, they become potential friends as well as potential romantic partners. Rex, for example, who has lived in a co-ed college dormitory for two years, says: "It was very educational for me to see women on a humdrum day-to-day basis—in the hallways, in the kitchen, in the bathrooms. Once you hear them worrying about their weight or insomnia or money, they just seem more human. They're not so different, so it's easier to be friends with them." When Rex first learned that he could live in a co-ed dorm, he imagined it would be some kind of nonstop orgy. He found, however, that most of his relationships with women in the dorm were simply friendships. Occasionally, these friendships would have a sexual side for a while, but this seemed very different to Rex from the romantic attachments he formed with young women outside the dorm.

Rex's casual attitude about his dormitory sexual friendships contrasts sharply with the attitude of his parents' generation, for whom "friendship" between a man and a woman could actually seem a failure. Friendship was something men of that generation settled for if the sexual scoreboard didn't light up.

Mixed-sex living experiences such as Rex's, whether in a dormitory or a shared household, not only de-romanticize the opposite sex but also open up new possibilities for friendly sharing of problems. Rex says: "When I'm having trouble in my relationship with Heidi, I can talk it over with one of my women friends here in the dorm. Since she's a woman, too, she can give me a new slant on what Heidi may be feeling or expecting. I can accept it from her because I'm not hung up on her the way I am on Heidi."

Since "recreational sex" is common among some young people, Bernie has decided that if he wants to be friends with a young woman, "It's best to get the sex out of the way at the beginning." He explains that if he is sexually attracted to a woman friend and knows she will probably sleep with him eventually, sex becomes the central issue for him, to the detriment of the other aspects of their friendship, which he knows are ultimately more important. Once they've gone to bed together, he says: "The mystery is dissolved, and we can relax and enjoy each other."

People who have been deeply in love often assume that should their romantic involvement end, their friendship will endure and the affection and understanding they've had for each other will continue to bind them together. In reality, however, even for people who separate amicably, seeing each other is too painful a reminder of what they once had and have now lost or turned away from. They may remain friendly, but only rarely can they remain true friends.

Yet, there is one category of former lovers whom circumstances compel to at least communicate with each other: ex-spouses who have had children together. Separating parents who share a genuine love and concern for their children will have not only the necessity but the opportunity to relate to each other warmly and supportively while promoting the children's welfare. Since children constitute a shared interest more powerful than most, and shared interests are a key to friendship, ex-spouses should at least be aware that it is possible for their relationship to be productive and pleasurable despite the hurts and disappointments of divorce.

Robert and Monica had been best friends who got married, had two children, and struggled with sexual incompatibility for six years. Finally they divorced. Neither blamed the other for their sexual problems; both were profoundly concerned about the welfare of their children; and both wished to preserve a healthy friendship. Consequently, they took pains to live within a few blocks of each other so that they could share the children in alternating two-week periods without disrupting their neighborhood friendships or school lives. Often they ate dinner at each other's house, since they continued to enjoy each other's company, conversation, and support as well. Once or twice they were tempted to "try again" with sex but soon abandoned the idea.

At first, Robert had a well-paying job, while Monica

brought in only a little money from part-time consulting work. As a result, Robert paid most of the expenses for both households. But in time Robert had to take a job ninety miles away and at a lower salary. Thus, the children spent summers and alternate weekends during the school year with Robert and lived with Monica the rest of the time. Monica soon was promoted to a better-paying, full-time position, which left her enough money so that she could occasionally send some to Robert. After two years, he was able to move back to town and again find a house nearby.

Throughout this time, Monica and Robert have maintained their many mutual friendships. They have a weekly potluck dinner, to which a group of six or eight come regularly with their own children. It appears that their friendship is stable and will endure indefinitely, though both are aware that it might change if one of them remarries or once their children are grown and leave home.

Faced with the complex interminglings of sex and friendship in today's society, some people conclude, as does Brooks, that friendship is inherently more valuable and more demanding than love. "You can go to bed with anybody, but you can't *make* a friendship happen," he says. "I'm a lot more willing to be most people's lover than their friend." Others feel that because both sex and friendship are valuable components of human relationships, friends ought to attempt to combine them.

Opposite-sex friendships will become a less difficult issue as people relate more as equals. Their gender will play a notably smaller role; and their likability, common interests, and shared impact upon the world rather than upon each other will all become more compelling than the merely sexual aspect of their relationship. Ideally, people should have the freedom to make the kinds of friendships they enjoy with the kinds of people they like, male or female, attached or unattached. We are the losers if we allow sexual considerations to limit our friendships.

8.

Friendship and Power*

Power relationships tend to inhibit friendships. People who fill inherently unequal roles—employers and employees, teachers and students, therapists and patients, social workers and clients—rarely become friends, though they may of course be friendly. We have found that real or imagined disparities in power make such friendships almost "taboo," perhaps because the higher-status person functions in a parental role vis-à-vis the lower-status person. Thus, we observe the curious fact that when a power relationship changes—the student graduates, the employee goes into another line of work, the patient terminates psychotherapy—people often feel free to explore the possibilities of becoming friends.

Jacob, an electronics executive, warns that mixing business and friendship is never wise. "If you do," he says, "you'll soon find yourself in drastic conflict between friendship considerations and business or professional ones. Friendship tells you to support your friend; your business interest may tell you not to. You end up betraying either your friend or your organization—and probably destroying the friendship no matter which way you go." Jacob also points out that people in management face

* In this chapter, we are not dealing with the power questions that arise within love relationships, though of course lovers do possess a unique power to hurt or gratify each other. We touch on such matters in our chapters "Mates and Friends" and "Sex and Friendship."

directly conflicting personality needs in their roles as executives and as friends. As managers, they are expected to be controlled, undemonstrative, competitive, and guarded about information and feelings. But these are precisely the qualities that inhibit friendship. As a consequence, many managers concentrate their friendship energies on people whom they know outside a business context, which minimizes their tendency to carry over managerial attitudes into friendships.

Another executive, Dora, has fewer qualms than Jacob about friendships within an organization, but she has found it best to limit her friendships to people in other departments with whom she is not in any direct competition. This policy, she feels, keeps her out of trouble and, as she adds with a grin, "has the side-effect of keeping me up on what's happening all over the company." Dora is naturally gregarious; and when she first joined the company, eight years ago, she attempted to cultivate friendships with people who were in similar positions in her own department. She soon found, however, that when a person is promoted, he or she tends to sever relationships with friends in the department, who suddenly become underlings.

Dora's experience parallels that of people in many kinds of organizations, where changes in relative status painfully affect friendships with "cohorts"—people in roughly the same situation. Employees who enter a company at the same time or struggle together on a common project often instinctively identify with each other as equals, fellow survivors. Often, friendship will follow. Such bonds, however, can erode with surprising rapidity.

Rachel and Jessica were good friends as long as they were both buyers in the same department store. They socialized together, often with other buyers, moved into the same neighborhood, and spent a good deal of time with each other both on and off the job. When Rachel was hired away by a supplier to work as sales manager for the region at a substantially higher salary, she felt vaguely guilty about leaving her friend behind and wondered if Jessica resented and envied her success.

Rachel also found herself looking at business from a different perspective. Jessica naturally expected that Rachel would do her certain business favors in her new position, such as occasionally giving her a break on prices. Rachel, however, was eager to succeed at her new job and was sensitive to possible criticism from her superior if she appeared to make undue concessions to buyers, especially if she knew them, as she did Jessica. Rachel and Jessica had several outright quarrels on occasions when Jessica felt that Rachel had betrayed their friendship; Rachel, on the other hand, felt that Jessica was making undue demands. Although they continued to do business together, though cautiously, it became increasingly difficult for them to do things together socially. Gradually, they grew apart. It was not until Jessica finally got a new job, in which she had no direct business contact with Rachel, that their friendship revived somewhat. But the status and monetary differentials have continued to limit the growth of their friendship.

While some people are prepared to go to some lengths in attempting to mix business and friendship, they must be able to distinguish professional duty from personal betrayal. Ross, a writer, says that rejection of his material by one editor who is a friend of his does not pose a serious problem for him. He has confidence in the friend's judgment, respects his publication, and knows that if the friend rejects a manuscript, he has sufficient reasons. This editor, after rejecting a piece, then switches to his role as friend and helps Ross either revise the piece or get it published in a more appropriate publication. Of course, as

Ross points out, this relationship is especially complicated because he and his editor-friend have done business together over the years, have worked together in professional organizations, and have come to know each other's strengths and limitations intimately.

Ross particularly appreciates this friendship because of another experience he's had. His friend, Clifford, a fellow writer, was appointed editor of one of the periodicals he and Ross had contributed to. Their relationship had been a cordial and egalitarian friendship—not a common thing among writers who, Ross says, tend to be prickly individualists. Before Clifford's appointment, he and Ross used to bounce ideas off each other, and read and criticize each other's work. They each considered the other a valuable colleague as well as a good friend. But almost overnight, everything changed. Clifford became inaccessible. He didn't return telephone calls; he stopped dropping by Ross's house; and he rejected several of Ross's contributions without comment or apology. Ross couldn't understand why his old friend was behaving this way. He attempted to set up an appointment with Clifford, but his secretary said Clifford was too busy. Finally, after many attempts, Ross reached Clifford on his now unlisted home phone. To his astonishment, Clifford shouted: "Listen, you bastard, if I want to talk to you, I'll goddamn well call *you!*" and slammed down the phone.

When Ross mentioned this episode to Patrick, another writer, he learned that Patrick had had a similar experience. Apparently, Clifford had decided that his newly acquired power required him to distance himself from his old colleagues. Ross believes that Clifford's guilt about his "elevation" over his friends caused this reaction, but that doesn't excuse Clifford in Ross's opinion. We suspect that another mechanism is also at work here. When Clifford "succeeded," he unconsciously expected Ross to adopt a submissive attitude toward him. Thus, by acting as if they

were still more or less equal, Ross unwittingly outraged
Clifford and so reaped his hostility as a result.

Not always do promotions destroy the friendship that
has developed between people who originally began their
relationship as cohorts. This was the case with June and
Dana, who were loan officers in the same bank. They had
lunch together from time to time and became quite
friendly. Their work relationship was finally translated
into a real friendship once the women began spending
time together outside a business context. They found with
pleasure that the majority of topics they discussed were
not at all work-related; and as time went on, they spent
more time together after work and on weekends. Even
after Dana was promoted to manager of another branch,
she and June continued to see each other. Because their
relationship extended far beyond the problems and concerns they had faced together on the job, their friendship
endured not only Dana's promotion but also their separation from the original situation that had nurtured their
friendship. June says: "If you go on seeing somebody after
they're no longer on the job, you know you're really
friends."

In general, there is something inherently isolating and
divisive about power. Especially in a traditional business
context, power cannot really be shared; hence, a power-
holder is sharply limited in relating to people over whom
he or she has authority. Yet, some people attempt to deny
the natural constraints against friendship in unequal
power situations. Hugo, a recently promoted supervisor in
an insurance company, thought of himself as a friendly
and democratic sort and attempted to "be human" with
his employees by exchanging confidences with them,
sympathizing with their complaints about work conditions, and explaining the reasons behind any orders he

gave. To his surprise, the employees responded guardedly to his friendly overtures, which even seemed to make some of them uncomfortable. Hugo finally sounded out Nan, the department's senior employee. Nan cautiously ventured that the employees felt Hugo was trying to pretend that the differences in rank between them and him didn't exist, but they knew they did. "So they don't know what you're up to, and they wonder if *you* know what you're up to. They can't trust you, and it makes them nervous."

Although Hugo made a few more attempts to treat his employees as if they were potential friends, he was forced to recognize that they would not, and perhaps could not, respond. Disappointed, Hugo realized that the managerial role he had accepted would preclude any great degree of intimacy with the people he supervised, however close they might have become in other circumstances.

Women employees are especially likely to be suspicious of apparently friendly behavior on the part of male superiors, since it is common for superiors to abuse their power by sexually harassing women workers, even to the extent of demanding sex in return for promotions or raises. Such men unconsciously justify this abuse of power with the belief that women are inherently unequal and thus fair game for exploitation—sexual as well as economic. A woman employee, therefore, may see an attempt by her male superior to appear "human" or friendly as a possible mask for sexual overtures.

Because of disparities in power in working situations, only in very special cases do true friendships develop between employers and their subordinates. However, this did happen with Ernest and Aaron. Ernest invited Aaron to join his New York corporate law practice because the firm was beginning to need the particular kind of international expertise that Aaron had. Ernest was highly regarded for having assembled other brilliant legal minds;

and Aaron, by strengthening the department, would further enhance Ernest's reputation. Ernest felt that it was unlikely that Aaron would become a threat to his own position; and he even sensed that the two of them, given their complementary talents and backgrounds, might become friends.

Both these assumptions proved accurate. In time, it became apparent that Aaron was, in fact, better than Ernest at the kind of devious financial finagling for which their firm received its immense fees. Although Ernest was nominally in charge, he would solicit advice from Aaron or ask him to help work out various problems; Aaron scrupulously kept these discussions confidential. At the same time, Aaron greatly admired and respected the fair, energetic, and organized way in which Ernest administered his department. The two men shared their avocational interests as well as their attitudes about their work, which enabled them to work together easily and pleasurably.

Not only did their work together prosper, but they found that they enjoyed each other's company after hours. Sometimes they would pursue their shared interest in old steam railroads; other times, they would seek out new or exotic restaurants.

Thus, the friendship between Ernest and Aaron was possible because they were largely able to sidestep questions of domination and vulnerability. Aaron did not exercise his potential for threatening Ernest's position; and Ernest encouraged Aaron to shine, hoping he wouldn't be lured out of the firm. The fact that they spent much time together outside the office ensured that their personal relationship would not be consumed by their business roles. Yet, if either leaves the firm, it will seriously test their friendship.

The many obstacles to friendship that exist within the usual business structure are fundamentally traceable to the fact that existing or potential power disparities inhibit friendship formation processes, which depend upon comfortable feelings of equality. A new business structure—employee ownership and control—has demonstrated widespread appeal primarily because under it, employees decide their own working conditions, wages, investment policies, and so on. But the egalitarian relationships fostered by this nonhierarchical structure also encourage the formation of friendships. Any employee-owned firm still has problems, as does any business organization, but they are dealt with in the context of direct personal relationships. Individuals who are truly equals, each with one vote in the operations of their firm, have opportunities for meaningful day-to-day friendship, which is one of the reasons we think employee ownership has a promising future.

Competition itself, paradoxically, can provide opportunities for the growth of a certain kind of bond. In business, as in sports, there is a thrill and excitement that comes from knowing you're up against a strong and determined competitor who will challenge your skill and judgment to the utmost. Especially in a small and highly competitive industry, the people involved come to know each other very well. They play tough—and not always fair—but there is a kind of intimacy in watching and countering each other's moves.

Power disparity problems are also acute, though genteelly concealed, in the academic community. Young, untenured faculty members often feel that unless they befriend the older, tenured professors who will someday sit in judgment on their tenure committee, they may remain academic migrant laborers the rest of their lives. Agatha, who has a reputation among students and faculty alike as a brilliant teacher and whose recently published book has been well received, worries whether these accomplishments will be sufficient for her to be granted tenure. "The pressure to barter toadiness for tenure is enormous," she says bitterly. The dilemma, as she sees it, is that even if she felt genuine friendship toward a senior professor, she might hesitate to express it, fearing to be taken for one of those who resort to toadying to compensate for their mediocrity.

Similarly, teachers' relationships with their students can never be truly equal, since teachers have the power to assign grades. Dale, a professor of cinema, has found this particularly vexing when he happens to have an unusually bright or creative student in class. "This one student," he said, "knew as much about gangster films as I did. And he'd come into the office to talk. We learned a lot from each other, but I still felt awkward. The knowledge that sooner or later I would have to give him a grade put a barrier between us. But if we'd met through the campus film club, we might have become friends." After the semester was over, Dale found he could communicate more comfortably with the student, but the origins of their relationship somehow clouded the possibilities for an egalitarian friendship.

Dale spends quite a lot of time outside of class with his students, socializing after film presentations. At the beginning of his career, he supposed that these informal contacts might lead not only to friendships but perhaps to romantic involvements. However, by observing cases where faculty members had become involved with students who were enrolled in their classes, he came to feel very strongly that such relationships were unprofessional and unacceptable because of their potential for exploitation. "For me," he said, "the essence of both love and friendship is freedom from constraint."

In the academic world, as in business, some people strive to avert the divisive effects of traditional power structures by organizing their work in egalitarian ways that will accommodate both work and friendship. Gail, Bonnie, Emma, and Melanie came to know one another as graduate students and shared the common pressure of preparing over a two-year period for an arduous master's degree examination. They devised ways of working together to cope with the vast amount of material they were expected to know, took mock exams together, and supported and encouraged one another along the way. After receiving their degrees, they found teaching positions in colleges in the same area and continued seeing each other. Remembering how well they had worked together as students, they wondered whether they could find a way to teach together. They spent most of a year researching a proposal for a course that would analyze creative works by women during the past four centuries, in literature, philosophy, music, and the fine arts.

Their proposal was accepted, and they plunged into preparations for the course. Their friendship made any potential work problems easier to deal with: they could agree on satisfactory working conditions, plan quickly and flexibly, shift responsibilities when necessary, and avoid any serious disagreements. The challenge of working together, they found, actually reinforced their friendship and brought them new understandings of each other's strengths and weaknesses. They helped each other work on their deficiencies, and all gained a great deal of self-confidence. The course was a success, and they are all pleased with the durability and obvious productivity of their friendship.

Power considerations also affect friendships among people not affiliated with the same organization or institution. In American society as a whole, real power resides in the ownership and control of productive resources; but this power's everyday effects on lifestyle are what mainly influence friendship patterns. In general, having markedly more or less money than someone else makes people uneasy because of the implicit power imbalance. No methods of coping with such imbalances ever altogether surmount them. But Irving and Pauline, a couple with a great deal of money, have made a consistent and fairly successful attempt to keep their economic good fortune from interfering with their friendships. They feel that this has been possible basically because they believe that being rich does not endow them with any special virtues, whereas most affluent people, they have observed, believe that their wealth makes them better than others. The rich who have inherited money, Irving and Pauline have found, are suspicious people on the whole who wish to associate only with persons of impeccable social connections and equal wealth; on the other hand, the newly rich tend to be so obsessed with their acquisitions and conspicuous consumption that they bore Irving and Pauline. Consequently, the couple tries to create an ambience, a "scene," in which they can gather friends around them with whom they are most comfortable. They are hospitable with their spacious apartment and country home, which they make available to friends for informal visits. Though they don't deny themselves some unobtrusive luxuries, they avoid an ostentatious lifestyle, which would put off the creative people they most enjoy associating with.

They have no friendships with people who are poor or with people who are intimidated by their money. Since they are selective about their friends, they rarely have a problem with people requesting loans. Through philanthropic projects they have occasionally become friendly with working-class people, but these contacts blossomed only into situational friendships that ended with the projects and were, in any case, clouded by the undeniable inequalities between donor and recipient. Irving and Pauline's closest friendships have arisen either with colleagues, who feel a professional equality with them, or with people who share other major life interests in which disparities in wealth can be submerged.

Another wealthy couple, Bruno and Nelly, are an exception to this pattern. They have opted to live in a modest style, and their close friends are mostly people they met in connection with their private, family life—as baby-sitters or housekeepers or craftspersons. Bruno and Nelly are connected with the art world and know many artists, art historians, critics, and gallery owners. But the couple doesn't feel comfortable gathering such people around the family circle; they prefer to see their art-world acquaintances elsewhere, quite literally keeping them at a distance. Their family friends are younger, lack money, and are thus rather dependent on Bruno and Nelly; however, though their relationships are not equal, they are surprisingly intimate. Reva, who has been part of their circle for the five or six years since she remodeled their kitchen, suspects that they prefer to have friends around who have no potentially corrupt relationships with the art world. "It's relaxing for them," she says. "They can just be themselves at home. If they have me over for one of their incredible dinners, I sometimes feel bad that I can't reciprocate. But they don't expect it—I'm just one of the family."

Although there is an implicit power relationship in any situation where money is at issue, Herman says: "A friend is somebody you would loan money to, and it wouldn't matter if you never got it back." In Herman's view, a real friendship commitment means standing by your friends even in adversity and giving their problems equal consideration to your own. Herman acknowledges that this is an idealistic position, but to him it distinguishes people who are real friends from those who are merely acquaintances.

Although Herman has lent money only in emergencies, Lila has accumulated enough savings so that she can extend herself financially to friends fairly often. However, she feels that lending money has less potential for damaging a friendship if a written agreement is made, stipulating when and how the money will be repaid. Although Lila's friends don't always rigidly adhere to the agreement, they feel that its existence clarifies this aspect of their relationship. They are usually more concerned about the loan than Lila is, keeping her informed about their plans for coming installments. Making the loan a "business proposition," Lila thinks, avoids vagueness that could generate guilt on the one side and resentment on the other, which would inevitably damage the friendship.

While generosity is a virtue, monetary gifts can have deleterious consequences for friendships. Carter, who came from an upper-middle-class family, lived a very modest student lifestyle with his wife, Stacey. Their friend Millie fell into difficult circumstances when her husband left her, taking their savings and leaving her deeply in debt. She was struggling to finish her degree, hold a part-time job, and pay off the debts when Carter came into an inheritance. Carter's generous nature and the guilt he felt at having received such a windfall led him to give Millie a substantial sum of money, which she accepted with relief and gratitude.

Afterward, however, Carter began to notice that his gesture had backfired and had jeopardized his friendship with Millie. Though she remained close to Stacey, she began to withdraw from him. She felt that Carter had put her impossibly in debt to him psychologically, breaching the feeling of equality between them; because she felt obligated to him, he became a patron rather than a friend. Carter gradually concluded that he had made a mistake and decided that he should have merely offered Millie a loan, with a clear agreement about later repayment, or perhaps just have given her a small amount so she would not feel demeaned after accepting it. Both Carter and Millie deeply regret the coolness that has come into their friendship but feel trapped by the situation.

In a society as competitive as ours, it is not only direct inequalities of power or wealth that inhibit friendship. Bradley, an ambitious Hollywood producer, is so concerned with his Mercedes, his apparel, his house at the beach, and the places where he is seen that he has little energy left for the simpler and more direct emotional contacts that comprise friendship. He compulsively injects status and power considerations into every relationship. As a result, he has no friends at all.

Some people are overly sensitive to any imbalance in their interactions with others and thus have a need to "keep score." The spontaneity and generosity essential to friendship are consequently destroyed when the focus is on who owes what to whom rather than on what might feel good to do. Reggie used to feel that only by rigid score-keeping could he avoid either being exploited by his friends or inadvertently taking advantage of them. A friend who found this behavior distasteful finally suggested to Reggie that his score-keeping seemed to indicate an inability to take real pleasure in things for their own sake. After some resistance, Reggie recognized the truth of the observation: his worries about who would pick up the check indeed prevented him from enjoying the meal. As a result, he agreed to experiment with not keeping tabs.

At first, Reggie was intolerably anxious when he tried to handle social situations without his usual calculations. However, after a few months, he realized to his surprise that things worked out fairly equally without his constantly worrying about it, and he was ultimately able to accept himself as occasionally being "unreasonably" generous or "dangerously" dependent. Best of all, he has found, when he doesn't try to control a situation, he is actually able to relax and enjoy it.

Other people who are inordinately sensitive to disparities between themselves and others may fall into the destructive habit of making comparisons. It is annoying when friends boastfully compare themselves to others, but it is even worse when that comparison is unfavorable to themselves. Perhaps they feel that a little self-deprecation will head off any possible competitiveness, or perhaps the ploy is a bid for sympathy or reassurance. Such exchanges produce a sense of unease about the relationship, since sympathy and reassurance feel valid to us only when they are freely given.

In certain circumstances, it is inappropriate to express these feelings. Courtney and Al had been college roommates but over time lost track of each other. Many years later, they ran into each other at a party. By this time, Al had experienced a meteoric political rise, while Courtney had stagnated in a civil-service position. Al was glad to see Courtney and inquired in a friendly way what he had been up to all these years. Courtney's failure to fulfill the bright hopes he had once shared with Al suddenly overcame him, and he could barely answer. Al persisted in being friendly and even invited Courtney to come by his office for lunch. But Courtney found, in the succeeding weeks, that while a part of him would have liked to renew the friendship with Al, another part felt hopelessly cast down by his relative failure and unwilling to have this sense of failure exacerbated by further contact. Al was not surprised by not hearing from Courtney; he had noticed often enough that many old friends had gradually withdrawn from him as he rose in prominence. And he recognized that there was nothing he could say to Courtney that would ease his pain of failure or restore the sense of equality that had prevailed between them as college friends. Power, as it so often does, had irrevocably come between them.

9.

Resolving Conflicts in Friendships

Some people feel that friendship is a natural phenomenon, like a waterfall. As long as there's water, its cascades continue; and if the water runs out, they stop. There's nothing you can do about it one way or the other. Other people believe, and we agree, that friendship, like other relationships, is an organic process which needs special nurturing and attention. A friendship may not always survive the effort invested in it, but we regard it as definitely worth a try. Of course, people vary greatly in the degree of attention and perception they bring to bear on their friendship patterns. Also, some of us are far more adept than others at resolving problems in friendships; and some people have trouble establishing meaningful friendships at all.

In friendship, as in love, human beings often behave in contradictory ways. Sometimes we may have difficulty telling an old and good friend some important personal news, while at a party we may confide our entire life story to someone whom we'll never see again. There are also times when the weight of an established friendship, which is both comforting and supportive, prevents new and exciting things from happening, and we seek out new friends with whom we do not have pre-established patterns of relating. Facing such ambiguous situations can be profoundly troubling and may lead us into questioning our own capacities for friendship.

This can happen, for example, when a friendship gets into a rut. Over time a friendship builds up meaningful "traditions" that both friends really enjoy—little things that make them feel at ease with each other. At the same time, some of these rituals may have degenerated into superficial, repetitive activities which neither friend finds rewarding any longer.

Cal and Gary have been friends since their college football days. Now in their thirties, their main shared activity is watching the weekend games on television and drinking beer. For some years this has suited both of them perfectly. Their families leave them alone, so they have the chance to swap stories, exchange impressions of the games, and generally take it easy.

However, the winter of Gary's thirty-fifth birthday found him taking stock of his marriage, his children, his job, his friends, his future. He wondered whether he was really making the contribution to society that he had thought he was capable of. And somehow, his weekend afternoons with Cal seemed to have lost their punch. He knew exactly what Cal was going to say; and instead of feeling good in a comfortable, familiar way, Gary began to feel bored and unstimulated. For a while, he did not act on his feelings but merely clung to the usual pattern, figuring that he'd begin to enjoy it again. But he didn't. He toyed with the strange and frightening thought that perhaps he was outgrowing Cal and that it might be all over between them. But since Cal showed no signs of dissatisfaction, Gary didn't even consider sharing his thoughts and feelings with him.

Gary finally decided that he simply had to take steps to get out of the rut, whatever the consequences to the friendship. As a result, one Sunday evening as he was about to leave for home, he told Cal that he wouldn't be coming around the following weekend because he'd decided to spend less time watching the games. As he had expected, Cal was surprised and a bit put out. Gary explained rather feebly that he had been meaning to do some projects around his house. While this explanation satisfied Cal for the moment, Gary knew that it wouldn't suffice indefinitely.

It happened that Gary had always had an interest in mushrooms. He was almost ashamed of it, really, but way back in high school he had become fascinated by their variety, color, and mysterious properties. So Gary decided to renew his interest by doing some reading and going mushroom hunting the following weekend. Encouraged by the success he had on his expedition, he attended a meeting of the mycological society in a nearby town.

Within the space of a few weeks, Gary felt much better about himself; he had met several interesting people at the meetings; and he somehow began to feel better about Cal. When he phoned and said he thought he'd come over again for a couple of hours on Saturday, Cal was pleased; and they both had a fine time. However, Gary refused Cal's invitation to return on Sunday. Because he was working to achieve a new balance in their friendship, he knew that he had to pursue his other special interests in his spare time, and not just sink back into his old routine. That way, he sensed, Cal would remain a lively and valuable friend to him. He was glad that he had taken the risk of alienating Cal and knew that he would do it again if he had to. It was only by retaining a certain independence

that he could make the friendship work the way he
wanted it to.

Because a friendship must, on the whole, be an equal
partnership, any serious imbalance that remains uncor-
rected can destroy the relationship. Of course, temporary
imbalances do occur; for example, one friend may be
needy at a point when the other is feeling strong. But if
one friend seems to be doing all the giving and the other
all the taking, the relationship will be either short-lived or
mutually destructive.

Sometimes what appears on the surface to be an im-
balanced relationship has hidden compensating factors;
but if you are a person who tends to develop unequal
relationships or feels that a friendship is taking a turn in
that direction, it is important to analyze the situation.
Usually, you can see what the other person is investing in
the relationship in comparison to what you feel you're
investing. Over the long haul, the inputs and outputs
should balance out. Also, beware of carrying the emotional load of the relationship, in some vague hope that
things will equalize later on.

Richard and Bob considered themselves friends and
spent a good deal of time together. Richard had been relatively successful and had recently inherited the family
business, which provided him with many contacts. Bob
was an attractive, intelligent, and dramatic figure, with
much to say about matters that deeply interested Richard.
He had also, some years earlier, had some experience in
the industry Richard was involved in. But he had tired of
this and had spent the last several years in an unsuccess-
ful attempt to become an actor. Now that he was down on
his luck, he was pressuring Richard to find him a job. He
did this by trying to make Richard feel guilty that he, his

friend, had to suffer the indignities of welfare and cheap
living while Richard ate in posh restaurants and was invited to wonderful parties. Richard also knew many interesting women, and Bob also pressured Richard—unsuc-
cessfully—to introduce him to them. When Bob was short
on funds, he appealed to Richard, who would occasionally
give him small sums of money, with the assumption that
he would never be repaid.

Richard was often provoked by Bob's incessant demands and wondered why he remained friends with a
person who caused him so much anguish—for he was very
vulnerable to Bob's accusations of indifference. It became
clear to Richard that unless something was done, he
would have to end the relationship. Yet, in some way, he
felt responsible for Bob and wanted to work on their relationship to make it more equal. Bob, too, was unhappy
about the way they related; he resented Richard's not
taking his life in hand, but at the same time he disliked his
own dependency on Richard.

As Richard tried to analyze the situation, he recognized
that he somehow must be contributing to the problem.
What, he wondered, was *his* payoff? He finally decided to
discuss it with another friend, who pointed out that the
relationship appeared to be a classic example of a giver/
taker friendship. He then suggested that the behavior Bob
indulged in, which Richard described as a burden, must
in reality be fulfilling some need Richard had. Bob's repeated cries for help were a pleasant reminder of how
well off Richard was by comparison. Moreover, the friend
suggested, Richard's rejection of Bob's pleas was a direct
way for Richard to exercise his power. And, of course,
from Richard's point of view, he could assure himself that
he was acting virtuously in Bob's own long-term interests
by forcing him to help himself. The friend also reminded
Richard that Bob's insight, warmth, and boyish charm all

had a real appeal for Richard, though in the current, rather tortured stage of their relationship, these qualities seldom had the chance to be expressed.

These perceptions helped Richard rethink the situation. He no longer saw himself as the upright, successful, responsible person dealing with a dependent loser. He realized with chagrin that he had actually enjoyed being the powerful figure in the relationship and had unconsciously encouraged Bob's subservience. As a result, Richard resolved to change the pattern. Whereas Bob had previously asked Richard to help him, Richard now took it upon himself to find ways in which Bob could help *him*. Bob was well informed about city events where Richard was not; consquently, he asked Bob to keep him up to date. Bob had a number of interesting artistic friends; Richard asked Bob to introduce him to them.

About this time, Bob found a job. Richard's feelings toward him had already been changing for the better, and Bob's employment accelerated the process. The two friends began to be far more comfortable in each other's company and in time were even able to discuss their past tensions with equanimity. Looking back, they could see a distinct and reassuring shift toward equality, which they determined to preserve thereafter.

Friendship is inherently a more honest relationship than love. When you deceive a friend, you are usually aware that you are doing something potentially destructive to the friendship, whereas in romantic love, the shared myth may become so powerful that many people think nothing of saying practically anything to preserve it.

Friends must be honest, but that doesn't mean speaking every angry or unkind thought, voicing every doubt, or reporting every piece of unpleasant gossip. Honesty does mean firmly stating your considered feelings, even when they may hurt or disappoint your friend. But friendship is also discreet; it requires common sense as well as a sense of timing. Also, friends soften the impact of hurtful comments by reassuring each other of their basic caring and concern. If friends systematically withhold feelings from each other or deny feelings or facts they know are there, they are, in effect, withdrawing from the relationship, and it will inevitably suffer.

Thus, most problems between friends require resolution, or attempted resolution, because ignoring them symbolizes the end of the intimacy that friendship demands. Yet, when minor irritations and annoyances arise, it may be best to carry on without making an issue out of them. A heart-to-heart confrontation, with attacks and counterattacks, every time a slight grievance occurs is a destructive waste of each other's time, energy, and affection.

When difficulties of consequence do arise in a friendship, it is important to remember that a basically sound friendship will endure, though a less placid period may be in the offing. People also vary enormously in their skill at confronting these kinds of situations. Some wear their emotions on their sleeve, others adopt an attitude of indifference. And some issues, which seem to threaten the whole relationship, are difficult to confront whatever one's emotional makeup.

People are often tempted to condone a friend's behavior even though they recognize the seriousness of the situation. After all, they reason, friends are supposed to be loyal and are not supposed to sit in judgment. But the fact remains that some friends really do need advice; and if you truly care about them, you should not refuse to offer it. To conceal your disapproval would be a betrayal both of them and of your convictions. If they have alcoholic tendencies or plunge into continual depressions or physically abuse their spouse or children, you are under no obligation to tolerate, and thereby tacitly encourage, their destructive behavior. If you steadfastly refuse to participate in or condone such behavior, making it clear that while you are fond of them you cannot accept what they're doing, it may help them realize the seriousness of their actions and lead them to seek professional help. There are also friends whose behavior is more subtly self-destructive, and there, too, you need to assert your own feelings in an open and frank way.

Sophia had known her friend Flo since they were 11 years old, though they lost touch for a while. When they re-established contact, Sophia couldn't help noticing that Flo only wanted to talk about her unhappy and uniformly brief love affairs with men. Sophia observed Flo's pattern attentively for some time and then told Flo that it seemed that she needed to repeat the same pattern of unsatisfactory and temporary relationships, and to recount them to Sophia in a way that had itself become boringly repetitive. More to protect herself from annoyance than to help Flo, Sophia finally said: "Look, I don't want to hear anything about any man unless you've been with him at least six months."

Flo realized that Sophia really cared about her and only said this out of desperation. She therefore took it very seriously and decided to make a concerted effort to change her pattern of relating. Somewhat to Sophia's surprise, Flo succeeded and has been grateful for the spur to her self-development, which Sophia administered out of her need for self-preservation. Sophia's angry refusal to hear more about Flo's misery probably helped Flo more than would have any amount of patient advice or insincere sympathy, which Flo could easily have discounted. Thus, we feel, there are times when *not* giving a friend what he or she seems to want and being true to your own feelings as well may be best for the friends involved and for the friendship.

There are limits to what friends should take from each other, particularly with respect to serious health problems. Mental illness, from which approximately one in every ten Americans suffers on a hospitalizable level sometime in his or her life, is one of these.

James is a victim of periodic depressions, which sometimes last several months. During these times, his friend Carl would find it extremely difficult to be with him. Without success, Carl would try to cheer him up by dropping by for a visit or inviting James out to the movies. Carl felt responsible for helping his friend, and saddened and puzzled by the fact that James had been, when he first met him, a cheerful and outgoing person. Now, he was in danger of losing his job (the two men were employed by the same company), and his other friends, sensing trouble, were backing off. Carl didn't understand the roots of James's troubles but thought they were connected to the loss of his woman friend some months earlier. When Carl talked to her about it, however, she said that James had experienced fits of depression before she had decided to break up with him. He had seemed bored with her, not terribly interested in sex, and unable to relate well with other people. One of the reasons she'd ended the relationship, she said, was James's quite angry reaction to her suggestion that he might need professional help.

Carl continued to reach out to James—though this wasn't much fun for him—because he felt that he was James's last link to normal life. He, too, suggested that James needed psychotherapy, since the depression didn't seem to be lifting by itself, and even gave him the phone numbers of several therapists. James didn't reject the advice outright; he simply ignored it and sank deeper into his depression.

Carl finally decided he couldn't deal with the situation any longer and stopped seeing James. One day when James failed to show up at work, Carl dropped by his apartment and learned from the manager that James had been found dead drunk in the hallway, incoherent, and had been taken to the hospital. Carl worried that perhaps their severed relationship had precipitated this crisis; but he also felt relieved that the matter was in someone else's hands—though he knew all too well that James's "treatment" would consist only of being pumped full of drugs.

The hospital experience shocked and alarmed James, and forced him to confront the dangerous mental state he was in. Shortly after his release from the hospital, he contacted one of the therapists Carl had mentioned. He then visited Carl at work; and though he was obviously still depressed, he told Carl that he was beginning to get himself together and thanked Carl for the support he had given him earlier. Carl was genuinely pleased about James's improvement, but he remained skeptical about whether their friendship would survive the pressures it had been subjected to.

Even aside from such major catastrophes, the course of friendship never runs altogether smoothly. No matter how dear two friends are to each other, there are bound to be conflicts, disagreements, misunderstandings; and unless these differences are confronted, they will inevitably seriously affect the quality of the relationship and may even destroy it. One friend may feel a persistent, nagging anger at another without being able to focus it on anything in particular. When this happens, we may begin to be especially critical of that friend. At these times, it is wise to remember that we often accuse others of failings which are not theirs but are rather projections of our own fears and anxieties. Thus, friends who are hellbent on the acquisition of material goods and very possessive of those they own may be suspicious of or offended by what they perceive as the excessive materialism of their friends. Or friends who are worried about their friends' loyalty may in reality be in doubt about their own. Perhaps the old adage "It takes one to know one" can serve as a reminder of this pervasive, indeed almost universal, projective mechanism. When we find ourselves ascribing some fault to a friend, even if we are prepared to forgive it, it is worth considering whether it actually lies within ourselves.

On occasion, we misread the needs of our friends. It is a temptation for friends—especially male friends—to assume that someone who is describing a problem wants practical advice about it rather than sympathy or understanding. As Ada puts it, when she tells a friend about the frustrations she is encountering in getting her subordinates to meet production standards, she isn't asking for an industrial-relations analysis; she wants to blow off steam and to have somebody pay attention to her feelings. Usually, the person recounting the problem is well aware of the available alternatives. Consequently, the effect of trying, no matter how sincerely, to give advice and help the friend solve the problem is to ignore the feelings that are being expressed.

Although Juan's friend Ramón doesn't offer advice, he is always ready to top a hard-luck story. If Juan returned from the racetrack having lost $120, Ramón would pop up with a story of the time *he* lost $200; if Juan ate something that disagreed with him, Ramón would tell him to be grateful he didn't have stomach cancer like two million less fortunate souls.

Friends like Ramón are usually under the impression that by distracting us with an even sadder story, they will make us feel better by comparison. Later on, we may be more receptive to the friend's gesture; but at that moment, what we really want is an attentive listener who is focused on *our* words, *our* experience, *our* pain. What we also want is understanding and sympathy, which can take the form of a wordless presence, a quick hug, a compassionate look, or any other direct response. We are not asking for a narcissistic attempt—misguided or unconsciously malicious—to minimize our troubles. Only when we ask for it should a friend offer his or her comparison, analysis, or advice.

On occasion, we also insensitively press our needs on our friends with total disregard of their response. While friends often are ready, indeed eager, to help out, there are times when, for reasons that seem valid and appropriate to them, they simply choose not to. Daphne went to Denver for a week with an old lover. This romantic tryst, however, did not work out after a few days; and Daphne, feeling rejected and rocky, badly needed another place to stay. Since she had rented out her apartment for the week she'd planned to be away and since she also had other matters to attend to in Denver, she decided to remain. She phoned Andrea, an old college friend who lived in the city, and asked if she could crash at her place. Andrea tried to signal that it was not a good time for her to have company, but Daphne persisted and seemed so needy and so oblivious to Andrea's lack of enthusiasm that Andrea finally agreed. Daphne arrived and stayed a few days. Andrea, however, was openly hostile and resentful that Daphne had not taken her needs and feelings into account. In fact, a one-year period of coolness ensued before they were able to make up and recapture the warmth of their previous relationship.

There are also small, annoying, infuriating things over which friends can become fiercely angry; after all, friends can "get to you" just as intensely as family or lovers.

Norma's friend Sean is a fascinating talker, full of wonderful if hard-to-believe stories, and Norma greatly enjoys his fanciful imagination. But perhaps because Sean doesn't regard the distinction between fantasy and reality as terribly important, he often makes promises he doesn't keep. Indeed, it sometimes seems that he never intended to keep them in the first place. Norma has gradually begun to feel critical of and angry at Sean, and these feelings have crystallized around Sean's promises to stop smoking. Norma understands that smoking (along with drinking) is part of Sean's social persona, but they both know that he has chronic smoking-induced bronchitis and runs an ever-increasing danger of developing a serious lung disease. Norma also has begun to interpret Sean's repeated promises to stop smoking, which he hasn't been able to keep for more than a day at a time, as insults to her, and she feels continually betrayed and let down.

Suppressed rage or resentment has a way of turning love relationships sour, and the same holds true for friendships. If Norma's anger is not expressed, it will probably inhibit whatever friendly impulses she may feel toward Sean.

Friends sometimes feel put-upon by a friend and tend to make excuses for the friend's behavior. But after a while, excuses don't work, and friends are forced to examine the behavior to see exactly why it is causing anger and frustration, to understand their own role in the interaction, and to figure out what can be done about the situation.

A relationship that fosters anger or frustration is not

giving either friend what it should. It may seem risky to bring the problem out into the open; and there are friendships which are so fragile or precarious that the acknowledgment of any difficulties may indeed cause a crisis. Also, because people are raised to avoid open conflict and to suppress or mask dissatisfaction, disagreement, or disapproval whatever the cost, it may be embarrassing or awkward for them to express these feelings directly and face the prospect of the friend replying in kind.

We believe, however, that friends owe it to themselves and to each other to surmount these hesitations and fears. Applying common-sense principles of conflict resolution to friendships makes us see that problems need to be resolved promptly rather than left to accumulate and fester. It's tempting to hope that problems will blow over, and sometimes they do; but the healthier course is to deal with them as they arise and never to ignore a friend's attempt to bring something up for discussion. The issue may not be a problem for *you*; but if it is for your friend, then it warrants confronting.

Once the cause of the anger and frustration has been isolated and identified, it can be looked at in an objective way. You are entitled to your opinions and feelings about even your closest and most valued friend's behavior, and you are entitled to state them clearly and simply to that friend. Of course, you need to listen to your friend's view of what is going on, but you are not obliged to accept it. It is also within your rights to insist that a friend stop or modify a behavior that is particularly irritating to you; and it is within your rights to ignore or refuse to respond to that behavior.

The method you use to resolve a conflict affects the outcome of the situation. Handling a conflict doesn't mean determining who's in the right and who's at fault. It does mean, however, frankly stating the issue so that the two people can reach a better understanding of each other; and unless both friends feel that their discussion has led to a just and fair compromise, both will lose, and the friendship will suffer.

When you wish to bring up a problem area, let your friend know that you value his or her feelings and understand that every person has an equal right to those feelings. Preface negative comments with an explicit acknowledgment that the friend's behavior in the problem area has some positive aspects as well. For instance, if you wish to straighten out misunderstandings with a roommate friend about the level of household cleanliness, you might begin by noting how you admire the neatness of your friend's closet or how she keeps her clothes in terrific shape. After that, she knows you are not simply out to get her, and she will be more receptive to discussing the dishwashing schedule or understanding your preference that she wash out the bathtub after using it. Preparing the foundation for dealing with problems by an initial good word shouldn't, of course, be done in a manipulative way —you should say only what you mean! But keep in mind that conflicts can be resolved only when both parties wish to resolve them. It may feel good to you to sound off, but if you begin a discussion in a way that precludes a cooperative approach and a sensible compromise, you will engender only resentment, hostility, and a continuation of the problem.

Another effective approach to conflict resolution is to begin with a quiet statement of your observation, asking your friend to listen to it and give you a reaction to it. This works better than charging in with an anger-provoking accusation. When Ellyn was feeling critical of the way Doug, her friend Karen's husband, failed to share in the household responsibilities and child-rearing practices, she began by saying: "I've been noticing that you seem to be doing all the cooking and housework and taking care of the baby, and Doug doesn't seem to be doing any of it. Is this the way you see it, I wonder?" Beginning in this way allowed Karen to present her perception of the situation. If Ellyn had simply attacked Karen at the outset, saying, "It makes me furious to see that you do all the housework and child care, and Doug doesn't do any," Karen would have been put on the defensive, and all her energy would have gone into refuting Ellyn's attack rather than addressing the real issues; and neither of them would have gotten anywhere in understanding the other's position.

When dealing with conflicts, you owe it to your friend and yourself to be full and explicit in stating your needs, feelings, expectations, and desires. Nothing is ever gained by accusing a friend of not knowing what you wanted. If your friend can honestly reply that you never conveyed this information to him or her, you may be acting as a dependent child and placing the friend in the parental position of knowing and fulfilling your expectations without being told what they were. This doesn't mean that if your feelings have been hurt you shouldn't point it out: "I really felt awful when you didn't see what I wanted." Made in a declarative rather than an accusatory way, such a statement will contribute to your mutual understanding, since it asks for sympathy, not an admission of fault.

Just as people in love relationships vary greatly in their capacity and inclination to directly and immediately confront and work out problems and tensions that arise between them, so friends do not always handle these matters as well as they might. Mary reports that she and her husband, who spend a great deal of their time together because they both work out of their home, can hardly go more than a few hours without attempting to grapple with whatever is bothering them. But with friends, it often takes longer. With one friend, Mary says, a pattern of conflict resolution has developed that, although effective in the long run, certainly has its drawbacks. Usually, the pressure builds up until Mary's friend becomes uncomfortable enough to lash out at Mary, who initially withdraws to avoid contact; then comes the realization for both that they must confront and examine whatever is going on, and they do. By now they both recognize the pattern and attempt to get through it as skillfully as possible. Although they can laugh about it, they wish they could deal with their irritations before their pattern of confrontation begins.

Henry and Rosanne, who have been friends for almost twenty years, regard fighting as a creative activity, a game with its own "aesthetic" rules. They like to make a lot of noise at it, going full out; but they also observe certain limitations about unfairness, about what would constitute "hitting below the belt." Even so, this process is harsh enough that other people sometimes can't take it—for example, roommates have moved out—and sometimes they overstep the bounds, which results in dangerous hurts that take time and effort to heal.

We advise friends to establish the ground rules for fighting before they begin. It's difficult if one person likes to argue quietly and the other likes to scream and yell; most successful friendships, like marriages, seem to be between people who operate at roughly the same "noise level." Ideally, you should set a mutually convenient time and place, where you will not be interrupted or overheard; define the area or agenda; and stick to it. You'll also need to establish areas of sensitivity which should be kept out of the discussion. It is important to confirm that you've understood the other's position *before* you respond. It is also essential, of course, to avoid physical violence. Some conflict-resolution experts do recommend maintain-

ing some kind of physical contact during the confrontation. Yet most people will probably find this more useful
in arguments with mates than with friends.

Constructive fighting has been made more difficult in
recent years by the focus on "total honesty," which can be
carried to the point of destructiveness. Some people argue
that discretion is a false, outmoded virtue, a kind of
hypocrisy. The result has been that kindness has taken
second place to a striving for truth—at all costs. In actual-
ity, these notions create a field day for people to attack
each other's vulnerable spots, to even old scores, and to
act out repressed hostility. Honesty between friends is like
any virtue: it is most valuable when tempered with judgment and compassion.

Some friends can carry on intense arguments which are
not fights but rather mutual, tough-minded explorations
of particular issues. What is essential here is the ability to
respect each other despite disagreement and to realize
that two minds may arrive at a conclusion sounder than
what either could have reached alone. Besides, the process by which two people really understand each other's
values and way of thinking can be intensely exciting in
itself; each person challenges and stimulates the other and
provides a sturdy test of the other's ideas and impressions.

While the failure to work at resolving conflicts often
leads to the gradual withering away of a friendship, it is
rare for friends to have an open conflict so severe that it
leads to a sudden blow-up and the severing of the relationship. As Amy exclaimed: "A good friend would *never*
do anything so outrageous that it would just end everything! We'd try to work it out." But there are situations
that simply prove too much for all concerned and certainly put a friendship in cold storage indefinitely. Warren and his wife, Marilyn, say that renting a houseboat
with another couple was for them a real test of friendship.

They had invited their old friends Pearl and Marv out for a week's expedition, to fish and relax on the sloughs and backwaters. Everything went wrong. Somebody mistakenly brought coffee beans rather than ground coffee; they got lost; the battery died; they threw the anchor overboard without attaching the rope; they lost the dinghy; the boat's propeller hit a rock and broke; and they had to be towed back to port. Suffering these disasters, with their emotional aftermath, in a total space only slightly larger than a bathroom, severely taxed the resilience of the friendship. As Warren puts it: "A time like that really shows who are the troupers and who are the crybabies."

Like everything else about friendship, trust is a two-way process. It is also projective; that is, trust *seems* to arise from the person trusted, but it really derives from the person doing the trusting. (The opposite case—people who are paranoiacally untrusting—makes this process more obvious.) The important consequence is that trust must begin with yourself. If you learn to trust yourself, you will extend that trust to others. This does not mean thinking of yourself as always doing the "right" thing. However, it does mean knowing yourself, including those areas in which you are not trustworthy, and acknowledging them.

When Erik was 22, he saw Ingmar Bergman's powerful film *Wild Strawberries*, which jolted him into confronting the absence of friendship in his life. Erik came from a Swedish background; his mother's family, particularly, displayed the same kind of bleak formality, distance, and rigidity in relationships that had destroyed the life of the old man, Isak Borg, in the film. Erik thus identified with the screen characters, and something about witnessing their abortive attempts at relationships forced him to recognize that he, too, had fallen victim to such unhappy, isolated ways of relating.

Many months of crisis, struggle, and painful self-questioning ensued. Erik found that old places meant a great deal to him—the scenes of his boyhood, for example, genuinely touched him—but people, even those who had been around him in childhood, meant very little to him. For some years, he'd been devoting himself totally to scholarship and saw human relationships as interruptions to his work; his infrequent contacts with women he felt were mere distractions. Racing along toward some ever-receding scholarly achievement, he abandoned ordinary human interaction, and he feels that he may have even used his studies as a defense against social situations in which he might feel awkward and unconfident.

A turning point came when Erik realized that before he could have friendships, he had to develop the confidence in himself which would give him a basis for trusting his reactions to other people. Slowly, this enabled him to extend himself to those whom he decided might be potential friends; and he learned to value how others extended themselves to him. Indeed, for Erik, friendship became "the ability to place value on what friends give you." Like Isak Borg, he concluded that realizing that friendship is a two-way street is half the battle for people who, like himself, have been caught up in mechanical, unfeeling, goal-seeking behavior.

The kind of confidence Erik developed is enhanced, for many people, by getting a firm sense of their own body, their own person, the solidity of their own being. We believe that psychic disciplines which involve body work—yoga, bioenergetics, *T'ai Chi*, meditational techniques that center you in your body—are most helpful for this purpose. Even sports can help; for instance, knowing that you can trust your body to run a seven-minute mile can be an important element in trusting it to "take care of you" in other respects. And, of course, anything that reduces your general anxiety level, from living in quieter surroundings to spending time with more relaxed people, is also a help.

A common fear in our society is that being trusting opens us up to terrible risks. Indeed it does, particularly because of the direct conflict between our notion that money is the ultimate criterion and motivation for human behavior, and our desire to be friends worthy of trust. Sophisticated people today may want to trust each other, but they are not surprised at being betrayed whenever monetary considerations make it worthwhile. This is both a debilitating way to live and another reason why we must somehow dethrone economic motivations from their commanding position in our society.

But even so, it is better to have trusted and been betrayed than never to have trusted at all. Without some degree of trust, human relationships wither—and friendships most of all. Thus, we owe it to ourselves and our friends, as well as to the future, to have the courage to trust—which, in the long run, can save us from the condition Hobbes describes as "the war of all against all."

We do not mean to suggest that even a long-established and precious friendship can always survive serious conflicts. Friendships sometimes end. But there is every reason for all of us to make strong, persistent, and serious efforts to resolve the conflicts that arise between us and our friends.

10.
Old Friends and New

Old friends are comfortable, known quantities; you can count on them. You have a common history, which provides a sense of stability and continuity. Old friends appreciate your strengths and accept your weaknesses. They've seen you through good times and bad; they've witnessed and shared your joys and triumphs, your sorrows and defeats. Old friends are your yardstick for measuring your changes: they "knew you when . . ."

But with old friends, however precious, the entire weight of the past is always present. As a result, it is important for you to remain open to establishing new friendships, which allow you to start with a clean slate. New friendships also give you the opportunity to concentrate on the process of "creating yourself." It's up to you to bring whatever you consider relevant from your past into new relationships. What's more, you're free to present yourself as you are *becoming*, not as you have *been*.

Wanda tends to seek out new friends who are rather like her or who complement her in some way. She appreciates people who are introspective, concerned with "what makes people tick." Most of her friends, she says, whether old or new, are people of similar tastes and outlooks.

Larry thinks it's a serious mistake to limit friendships to people who are only like ourselves. In his experience, much of the stimulation of new friendships has come from the fact that new people pique his curiosity and challenge his views and attitudes. He points out that because they operate differently from him, he is exposed to other ways of thinking and of looking at the world. He has new and unusual experiences, some of them leading him into adventures he wouldn't have had otherwise. Larry feels that these friends also add to his understanding of the ways in which people adapt to the world, which gives him new options to consider for his own life. He says: "The more different people I know, the more I feel I understand human nature. It sharpens my sensitivity about others and keeps me alert."

In general, people are initially attracted to each other on levels apparent to casual observation: physical appearance and attributes such as warmth, sensitivity, energy, humor, emotional style. Then, as people get to know one another, a more complex evaluation takes place, focusing on processes of interaction—mutual acceptance, spontaneity, loyalty, support. Above all, people explore the possibilities of the exchange of feelings, that half-conscious process which determines psychic compatability, the degree to which people will be able to see into each other's beings and express their kinship.

On another level, people form an impression of whether a potential friend's mind works in a way with which they feel comfortable. This is partly a matter of intelligence; we rarely choose as friends people we consider either markedly more or less intelligent than ourselves. But it is also a matter of education, class and lifestyle, and personality type. Some people think and talk in a playful, spontaneous way and are happiest when they find themselves with people who are always coming up with original thoughts and clever remarks. Other people are more low-key and serious, and are most at ease with people like themselves. It's important to remember that you are entitled to your own taste in friends; nobody's preference is "better" than anybody else's. You may want friends who stimulate you; you may want friends who sustain you; you may want friends of both kinds.

People also intuit a potential friend's level of experience and sensitivity when they first meet, and respond most positively when they recognize a kindred spirit who, they feel, must have suffered similar trials and who must appreciate similar pleasures. Subsequently, of course, these intuitions may prove to be incorrect.

When Bart first met Jesse, he enjoyed Jesse's caustic, iconoclastic spirit. They shared many laughs at the restrictions of bourgeois living and at the corruption of politics and business. Gradually, however, Bart became uncomfortable as he sensed that Jesse's disenchantment with society went far beyond his own. He began to wonder where Jesse, who was not regularly employed, got his money; at the same time, Jesse took to mocking Bart's devotion to his work, which embarrassed Bart and put him on the defensive.

Shortly after their friendship began, they had dinner together at an expensive restaurant, where they ran up a rather large bill. Jesse said he'd take care of it while Bart went to buy cigarettes. After they had left the restaurant, Jesse clapped Bart on the back and welcomed him to the criminal classes: "We just stiffed them for forty bucks, man!" This was considerably more than Bart could handle in the way of anti-bourgeois attitude; and though part of him envied Jesse's outlaw sensibilities, he severed the incipient friendship.

People also make judgments and assumptions (though not always accurate ones) about a potential friend's intellectual prowess, social connections, and sexual sophistication. If they sense significant disparities in these areas, they may feel that the imbalance will seriously hamper the relationship. The danger here is that by categorizing other people narrowly, or by categorizing ourselves in respect to others, we prevent ourselves from seeing others as individuals, and thus may turn away from potentially interesting contacts.

Emily believes, as we do, that people tend to have "open" periods during which they are ready to establish new friendships, and other periods when they are not. Just as people give off subtle, nonverbal signals indicating whether or not they are open to sexual approaches, they also communicate—often through nonverbal means— whether or not they are open to overtures of friendship. Some people give the impression, "I'm really self-sufficient and not open to or interested in relating to you," while others indicate, by words or actions, "You can approach me, I won't judge you harshly, maybe we can be friends."

Emily has also observed that her own openness for friendship increases during times of danger or risk, when she is throwing herself into new situations and coping with new challenges. If her patterns are disrupted, she becomes ripe for new contacts, reaching out in ways she often doesn't when her life is steady and settled.

In order to be open to new friendships, you must be willing to occasionally take the initiative. If you do not seize the opportunity to indicate to another person that you'd like to get to know him or her, the possibility may well pass by, and both of you are likely to be the losers. You also need to be a bit persistent. Michael says he has adopted a rule of thumb: he gives a potential friend two chances and always provides a diplomatic way out if the person doesn't wish to pursue the relationship. If Michael's first invitation is refused, he doesn't press with possible alternatives; he just drops the subject. A week or so later he calls back with another invitation. If that one is also refused, Michael concludes fairly reliably that that person isn't really open to getting to know him better.

Approaching a potential friend can make you feel vulnerable, since you may be rejected. An offer of friendship is also an act of trust; and what we take to be our fear of rejection from outside may be a lack of trust within ourselves, which we are projecting onto others. Coming to know your own feelings and acknowledging the negative side of them are essential to the development of self-trust, which will give you the courage to risk exposing yourself.

Most of us, though we often don't realize it, are presented with new and potentially intriguing contacts every day. It's easy to overlook the role proximity plays in the generation of friendship. People who are thrown into each other's company simply by being neighbors, riding in the same bus or carpool, having children in the same class, or working in the same company can often make the leap from mere association into friendship. Never dismiss such contacts; if you remain open, some of these relationships may blossom and surprise you.

It's also important to remember that people are not always what they seem. A woman who looks as if her main exercise is pushing the elevator button may turn out to be the lunch-hour running partner you've been searching for. A conventional-looking business acquaintance may turn out to be a serious painter who would be delighted to share your studio. It may be unsettling at first to consciously invest time and effort in sharing yourself with potential friends, but you will improve with practice and learn that there's a certain excitement in exploring others.

While some people have difficulty expressing their emotions as openly as they would like, they occasionally break through to potential friends in unexpected ways. May was unable to tell her new friends Brenda and Stan how much their friendship was coming to mean to her. Very late one night she phoned them and said: " 'Scuse me. I'm down here at the laundromat and really drunk, watching my clothes spin round and round, and I just had to call you and tell you what neat people I think you are!" Brenda and Stan, though groggy, were deeply touched by May's attempt to reach out.

On another occasion, some casual friends downright astonished them. They had met Martin and Georgia because their children were enrolled in the same gymnastics program. Martin and Georgia seemed to be ordinary, community-oriented, churchgoing people, though by Brenda and Stan's standards they were a little reserved and socially awkward. The two families often went out together for pizza after gymnastics events, and the acquaintanceship developed slowly but steadily. Because Martin and Georgia seldom revealed much about their attitudes and feelings, Brenda and Stan were especially pleased when they were invited over for dinner and home movies.

After dinner, Martin and Georgia set up the projector and screen, served coffee, and turned out the lights. Brenda and Stan were amazed to see that the home movies were of Martin and Georgia's vacation—at a nudist colony! Even more surprisingly, Martin and Georgia said not a word in explanation but merely commented in a matter-of-fact way on the scenic beauties of the place and the interesting people they met there. Brenda and Stan felt somewhat inhibited about asking questions and concluded that Martin and Georgia had shown them the films as a kind of substitute for the self-revelation which most people carry out through conversation; it was a way of quite literally "showing themselves."

There is a pace of mutual self-disclosure in friendship that is proper and comfortable for any two persons, and you need to be sensitive to it. Some people, convinced that self-revelation is the essence of friendship, go too far too fast and embarrass potential friends, who subsequently withdraw. Even if you feel a special bond of empathy between yourself and someone you've just met, you should ordinarily refrain from immediate, intimate revelations about your history or character. Let the potential friend get to know you by seeing you in action; it's not necessary to explain or justify yourself to anyone.

Though most friendships take a long while to develop, Bibi insists that she knows within an hour of meeting someone whether they can be friends. "It's like falling in love," she says. "You know if the potential is there, even though sometimes it develops slowly."

You certainly do not make new friends by sitting around waiting for someone to coax you out of your apathy or shyness. Consequently, people who are looking for new friends will usually remind their other friends and acquaintances of their desire to be invited to dinners and parties and other social events. But we have observed that the single most important strategy for finding new friends is to concentrate on your own real interests, which will open up new possibilities for relating to new people. Nothing makes you so attractive as being engrossed in some activity that truly engages your talents and intelligence.

But the pursuit of interests, new or old, must flow out of what is genuine and permanent and valuable in yourself; they must be things that would matter to you whether or not they were connected with friendships. People are very quick to sense whether you are interested in something for its own sake. If you're not, they will be suspicious of you; but if you are investing your positive energy in some project or interest that is meaningful to you, others will respond to this energy, not because you ask them to but because it feels natural and good to them.

Sometimes you face the difficult situation of discouraging someone who is trying to develop a friendship with you. We know no way to do this with grace and equanimity. Most people first try a simple failure to reciprocate; but this sensible technique often doesn't work: a persistent person may continue to phone you, extend invitations that are awkward to refuse, or create embarrassing situations where open rejection seems your only course. If the person refuses to take discouraging hints, you should state your feelings on the matter clearly and openly, leaving the door ajar for possible future contact only if you sincerely mean it and not merely as a sop to your pursuer's feelings. This bold course is difficult. Eva was being approached persistently by a woman who hoped to become her friend. After much hesitation, Eva told her frankly: "I'm really sorry, but I just don't have time for you." The woman was cut to the heart. But Eva still feels, and so do we, that her action was kinder than stringing the woman along indefinitely with excuses, which might have allowed her to keep up false hopes that Eva would in time be available. Honesty in these matters may not be easy, but in the long run it is the more humane and helpful approach.

It may be so obvious that it hardly needs saying, but in order to become friends, people must spend time together. Once a friendship is well established, of course, it may survive periods of neglect. But in its earlier stages it needs nurturing if it is to develop into a serious friendship. A person who is heavily scheduled or very cautious with time commitments is likely to give others the feeling that they are being sandwiched in between more "important" things. They usually will conclude that the person is not really interested in being friends. The tightly scheduled person may respond to this with surprise and hurt, and may accuse the friends of not understanding and of making undue demands. When two people have sharply different ideas on this subject, it's often impossible for them to work out a deep or easygoing friendship.

Friends are people who spend time with each other simply because they enjoy each other's company. Yet, few friends spend enough time together that is unscheduled or unstructured, allowing for spontaneous developments, following up of impulses, or doing nothing much at all. Some of the most rewarding and beautiful moments of a friendship happen in the unforeseen open spaces between planned activities, and it is important to allow these spaces to exist. This consideration is especially important for people who devote large blocks of time to their spouses, families, or lovers, and who may otherwise restrict their outside friendships.

Contemporary life offers too few relaxed opportunities for random contacts of the sort that encourage the formation and continuation of friendships. We lack the pubs where a great deal of British social life is carried on; we lack the neighborhood cafés of the Mediterranean countries; and churches, although they provide small towns and a segment of our urban population with a place to congregate, are not the centers of community life they once were. In fact, it is mainly on residential college campuses that people find ample opportunities for informal contact; and it is no accident that many long-term friendships begin during the college years. Students typically have little ready money and little occasion to exercise their talents in real-world occupations, so they have plenty of time for friends; later, a trade-off occurs, and they usually have more money, a busy work life, but much less time to share with friends. It is a rare person who achieves a satisfying balance; most of us oscillate, more or less unconsciously, from one extreme to the other.

Leroy recognizes this problem and attempts to deal with it by limiting the time he is willing to spend on a job; he usually works part-time and at irregular jobs, and even relies considerably on unemployment, because of the importance he attaches to spending time with his friends. "I enjoy my friends more than I'd enjoy making more money," he says, "and I have plenty of free time, so I can be ingenious about saving money for the things I really need. In fact, my friends tend to be people who also get kicks from seeing how economical they can be."

Lynne, on the other hand, is a workaholic. She has a demanding full-time job in advertising, which involves long and irregular hours, as well as some weekend work. She also contributes her time and energy to a small, struggling public-interest media organization (for which she doesn't get paid). She does this in the evenings and occasionally on weekends, and it is gruelling, draining work.

Both Lynne's friends and lovers find it difficult to cope with her schedule. She tends to be "booked up" weeks ahead and is extremely reluctant to change business appointments once she has made them. Some of her friends feel that this puts them in an uncomfortable "controlled" position, since it is always Lynne who, with the excuse of pressing appointments, decides when and where and how they will see each other. One of her former friends remarked: "I felt like I was dealing with a secretary who had been instructed to keep people out of the boss's way." Others have learned to live with Lynne's schedule but only by realizing that they have to plan anything they want to do with her several weeks in advance.

Lynne, and others like her engaged in relatively altruistic pursuits, may cripple their friendship lives by an over-commitment to work. Still, their friends, realizing the basic good-heartedness of the impulse driving them, may do their best to adjust to the situation and hang on. More frightening are those for whom business is an all-encompassing passion in itself. There really are people who have been known to talk business on the phone and make love simultaneously. It is small wonder that their friendships suffer—if indeed they ever allow themselves to have any friendships at all. There is something about the "hunger" of ruthlessly ambitious people which scares away potential friends. Facing someone with such an indiscriminate hunger for business, potential friends may fear that they too could easly be gobbled up.

There are also people who are so immersed in their sex life that they have little time for friendship. Dick, who had recently gotten divorced after a long and unhappy marriage, was having great difficulty finding time for his friends—both those old friends from his married days and new people he was trying to cultivate. Single, employed, and reasonably attractive, Dick found himself extremely popular with women, from whom he was constantly receiving invitations. His social calendar was so crowded with appointments that his friends found that he had no time for them; and when he finally did make himself available, he would bring along his latest lover, whether or not the friend had invited her. In time, the situation became intolerable for most of his friends.

Finally, an old friend persuaded Dick to join a men's group, which had, as one of its ground rules, compulsory attendance at every weekly meeting unless the member was bedridden. Absenteeism for work, depression, or other reasons was unacceptable; and absenteeism in order to be with a woman was simply unthinkable. Dick was astounded when he heard this, since he had been in the habit of making his sex life his number-one priority and permitting nothing to interfere with it.

The group's members came down hard on Dick and made him see that there was something compulsive about his sexual exploits, as if he were using them to blot out the bad experiences he had had with his wife—which he realized was partly the case. He also saw that it was an insult to his friends to constantly expect them to take a back seat to his relationships with women.

Gradually, Dick began to restrict his dates with women to three or four nights a week and to devote some of his free time to his men friends; he even developed a strong nonsexual friendship with a woman. But he preserved his exciting and varied sex life, which he realized was partly a way of making up for lost time.

Very outgoing people are sometimes unavailable because they are always with someone else. Some such individuals have the syndrome we call Too Many Acquaintances, Too Few Friends. Dave is an organizer for an international union. His work requires that he travel a lot, and he rarely spends more than a week in any one city. He has acquaintances throughout his territory, and many of them drop in on him when he is in his hometown. But these acquaintances have discovered that it's almost impossible to tie Dave down to an appointment unless it is business-related. In his restless way, he's always "keeping his options open," as he puts it. Dave formerly lived a settled, married life but found it didn't suit him. "People were always expecting things of me that I couldn't give," he explains. "Living the way I do now lets me do things that seem worthwhile to me, but I don't owe anybody anything." Yet Dave is seldom alone; his life is peopled with a huge assortment of associates who like him well enough on the limited basis he allows: here today, gone tomorrow. There is no room in his life for a serious friendship or a serious love affair, which would require a deep commitment to one individual, something Dave has always consciously or unconsciously shied away from making.

Couples going through the early child-rearing years are usually hard-pressed to find time to pursue their friendships. Children's demands on their parents' time severely restrict the amount of time parents have for themselves; and if money for babysitting is tight and relatives or friends are not easily available to care for children, the tendency to become homebound is that much stronger. As a result, out of convenience parents may limit their friendships to people who have children of the same age: the children can play while the adults socialize.

We feel that it is dangerous to become too home-centered in this kind of situation, especially for the parent who stays at home most. There's a loss of stimulation, excitement, and variety in life; and couple problems, in this pressure cooker, can easily get out of hand. The fact is that these are the years when you really need friends the most, though you may find them the hardest years in which to set aside time for them. So it is important to make a real effort to maintain old friendships and develop new ones; out of them you will gain the strength to deal with the grinding problems of early parenthood. Even if it means leaving your children behind when you might like to have them with you, it's crucial to continue an independent adult life with activities where children are not present. Children are not the only people in a family who need to grow.

George and Audrey, a couple in their thirties, became conscious of this problem. They have children; they both have jobs; and they are involved in city politics. They have many associates in these various areas of their lives who occupy their time quite fully. As Audrey says: "Sometimes people approach us—invite us to dinner, say —but somehow we don't seem to find the time to reciprocate. We let opportunities slip by and just don't make an effort." They are aware that they should put more effort into their friendships, and they intend to do so once their children have gotten a little older. But this is a priority that is easily neglected, as we often put friendship in a subordinate position to family or business.

Although some people seem to have time they could devote to their friends, they may decide to spend a great deal of it alone. Penny is one of these people. She loves to spend her evenings curled up with a book or magazine, and she invests much of her other spare time in running. Both are best for her as solitary activities.

Some of her former friends found it difficult to understand why, if they invited her to dinner or to a movie or to a concert, she would sometimes reply: "Thanks, but I think I want to go on with my novel tonight." The reason is that some people need more emotional "space" around them than others and feel crowded if they are subjected to the amount of human contact with which most of us feel comfortable.

Penny's friends understand her and don't press her to join them when she wants time to herself. They've learned that if they honor her need for space, she is lively and warm and witty when she does want company, whereas pressing her only leads to tensions and misunderstandings. She is definitely not one of those people who want to be coaxed. She genuinely wants to be left alone sometimes, and she manages to find friends who respect this and love her nonetheless.

·   ·   ·

People must make not only time for their friends but also space; that is, they must open their living spaces to their friends. One criterion for whether a relationship is a real friendship or not is simply whether two people spend time in each other's homes. If a person never crosses your threshold physically, it usually means that he or she has not crossed your threshold emotionally either.

Wayne and Maureen had been getting to know Roberta; but at the time, they were moving into a new neighborhood and decided they didn't want to pursue the relationship, though they continued to run into her at parties. That New Year's Eve, she called up, drunk, to berate them. "You've never once invited me to your new house," she said, "and I think that stinks!" Thus, inviting someone into your home is a clearly understood signal that you are interested in letting the relationship become closer. It doesn't matter whether it's for dinner, drinks, to watch television, or just to assemble before going out; opening up your space is what counts.

While most of us face the problem of being sufficiently open to new friendships, there are people who, at first, appear to be enviably open and who rush into relationships with great enthusiasm. This, however, can prove to be difficult for their prospective friends to handle. Paul and Susanne, who felt they were themselves quite open to new contacts, met Charles at a party and were taken with his vivacity, charm, and energy. He was intelligent, attractive, and ambitious; though only in his early thirties, he had held various government and university research positions and was already well established in his field.

Over a period of several weeks, Paul and Susanne thoroughly enjoyed Charles's company. They invited him to a concert, and the following day he brought by a recording of a quartet that had especially moved them. He invited them to a festive gourmet dinner at his home. And he spoke constantly—a bit too constantly, they felt—of what a delight their friendship was to him. He would talk about how they would all get together in far-away places and how pleased he was that their friendship was going to endure through the years. When he invited them to join him for a weekend at a beach house he had rented for the summer, they enthusiastically accepted.

Charles cooked one of his fabulous dinners. There was champagne and wine and liqueurs. Charles revealed some spicy details about his past sexual exploits—he had never married and his wandering lifestyle had led him into many bizarre encounters—and shared his deepest ambitions and fears with them. It was a warm, intimate evening; and the next day, when Paul and Susanne were getting into their car to return to the city, they both gave Charles a big hug. "You know," Paul said, slamming the car door, "we're really happy to be friends with you."

After that, Paul and Susanne were surprised to find that unless they initiated contact, they saw nothing of Charles. Sometimes he would phone and say how fond he was of them, but it would somehow prove impossible to work out a mutually convenient time for them to get together. Paul and Susanne became increasingly suspicious. Whereas before Charles almost always had time for them, he now was either involved in an intense but brief love affair or was working until the wee hours on some important project or was exhausted from the infighting at work.

Paul and Susanne gradually learned that not only were Charles's love affairs short-lived but his friendships were also. He might describe someone as a dear friend, and it would later turn out that he hadn't seen that person for several years. Charles's ability to talk intimately about his sex life or other personal matters, yet somehow keep his own present feelings safely at a distance, made Susanne uncomfortable. Paul felt somewhat the same; he also had the impression that Charles saw friendship as an "I—I" relationship: the "thou" was missing.

In time, Paul and Susanne came to dread Charles's calls, which always began with a restatement of his devotion to them, yet ended so inconclusively. The relationship drifted into a state of limbo. Paul and Susanne sometimes wondered whether the failure of the friendship was their fault, or Charles's, or the result of some mysterious interpersonal "chemistry." But as far as they could tell, this was not a question that agitated Charles. He was already involved in the courtship phase of yet another brief friendship.

We call what happened to Paul, Susanne, and Charles a skyrocket friendship: a fascinating, exciting relationship that somehow fails to develop into real friendship. People like Charles can be intriguing—until their friendship campaign succeeds in eliciting an expression of commitment from its object, at which point they lose interest. In this, Charles may have unconsciously been following "scripts" laid down for such quick and transitory relating by the stories prevalent in our fiction and television: each of his truncated attempts at friendship constituted a new "episode" in the serial of his life.

People exhibiting this seductive kind of behavior avoid exposure of their real selves. They take satisfaction instead from repeatedly breaking through a new friend's natural shyness and reserve. Their sexual relationships may tend to follow the same pattern of early over-intensity quickly followed by indifference; they may never marry, or marry often and briefly.

Of course, such abortive friendships are frustrating on both sides. While Charles was still pursuing them, Paul and Susanne seemed to be the true friends he was seeking. But once they had openly committed themselves to him, he lost interest, and even his protestations of friendship sounded unconvincing. The very intensity of his grasping at them betokened deep doubts of his own worthiness as a person to whom others would naturally turn in time without being emotionally pressed. Charles needs to learn how to develop friendships at a slower pace, allowing intimacy to build step by step, with mutual challenge and response, mutual self-revelation, and a slow, unforced growth of confidence and trust.

Brief but intense friendship-like relationships arise when people find themselves in situations that separate them from their daily routines of work and family. Encounter groups devoted to personal growth, business-training sessions, conventions, religious retreats, and intensive educational workshops often turn out to be remarkably powerful experiences. The intensity of concentrating with a close group of other human beings on practically any subject—from personal problems to plans for new enterprises—generates a reflection of energy back and forth which is strong enough to bring most persons to a distinctly heightened emotional state, where they become unusually receptive to others' ideas, personalities, and values.

Ordinarily, people who participate in events of this kind report at the end that although the experience may have been insight-producing, stimulating, tiring, or infuriating, they found through it a wonderful sense of companionship and human warmth; they anticipate that they will stay in touch with the new people they met and become real friends. However, this seldom happens once they leave the artificial world of the event and return to the pressures and demands and complexities of their regular lives.

Threatening situations can cause a similar closeness to

spring up between people. Being involved in a crisis—an accident, a hijacking, a power blackout—can cause a burst of fellow feeling with people you don't know. And, as Marcel reflects on his river-rafting experiences: "Doing something really dangerous together makes you evaluate your companions very carefully. If you get through it successfully, the members of the group feel a lot of trust and affection for each other, whether they have much in common or not." The bonds forged in dangerous activities such as rafting or mountain-climbing may transcend differences in age, class, or nationality; and in some cases, they may prove quite lasting.

On the other hand, as Leonard remarks, recalling his experience of being stranded for several days by a hurricane in Guatemala: "You think after you've gone through something like that together that you'll always keep in touch. But somehow, the original stimulating situation just loses its force. You stop writing those letters and maybe feel a little guilty—or angry that the others are not coming through with them either." Such disaster-engendered friendships seldom have the enlivening effect on their participants' lives that they had anticipated.

Foreign travel, particularly when people are thrown together quite randomly on a cruise or group holiday, often engenders the development of surprisingly strong ties. The enforced contact with each other and isolation from "normal life," the disruption of their ordinary routine, their mutual dependence on impersonal others for food and other necessities, the strangeness of their surroundings and experiences, all contribute to their connecting with each other in ways they ordinarily wouldn't. The freedom from restrictions, community standards, and other inhibiting forces also makes many people more friendly and more open on vacation, allowing intimacy to grow rather quickly.

Conversely, Americans are often hospitable and emotionally open to foreigners who are visiting here, and sometimes exciting but short-lived friendships result. The foreigner may well be in the receptive stage just described, and to the American partner in such a friendship the foreigner may have the special appeals of the exotic or of the stranger in need of help. The foreigner also offers the challenge of new perspectives, and the fact that the friendship cannot last very long adds piquancy to it.

We think it is best to recognize, regretfully, that such relationships, however warm and open, will not necessarily lead to full friendships. It is unwise to mourn such flashes of intimacy; they're like mountain wildflowers that bloom only in hazardous locations and must be enjoyed in their brief season. For some people who don't have partners or long-term friends, these transient contacts are something to look forward to; they are friendships in miniature, with few demands or responsibilities.

New friendships often disrupt old ones—to their benefit or detriment. Old friends may not be terribly pleased about your making new friends; they may see it as a reflection on the kind of friend they have been, or they may be jealous of the time you are now spending with someone else. It is also true that new friendships cause you to look at your old ones from a different perspective. All the same, you'll feel protective of your old friends; after all, they've been long-term figures in your life, and it isn't easy to admit that there *are* things about them which you find irritating or distressing. While friendships sometimes develop between old and new friends, this isn't usually the case; and you'll find that it's best to spend time with them separately.

Shared interests are the foundation of many new friendships. But it also happens that a person will develop a passionate new interest and through it temporarily or permanently alienate old friends. Sheila and Pamela had been close for many years. When Pamela went to graduate school, she fell in with a new circle of people, all psychologists, who lived, breathed, and talked nothing but psychology. Pamela, urgently trying to establish herself in this new world, immersed herself in their conversation and lifestyle.

Sheila was a person of broad interests, and she felt Pamela's new life was limiting her intellectual horizons. For a time, she made valiant efforts to get Pam's mind off psychology—at least for brief periods—but to no avail. She then took to avoiding Pam, expecially when she was with her psychologist friends. Finally, however, she realized the matter had to be brought into the open. "You know," she said, "I have to confess that talking nothing but psychology bores me silly. I still love you, but I can't stand spending all our time this way. So I've decided to just call it off for a while, take a vacation. I'll be there if you need me, but let's just give the friendship a rest."

Pam was astounded. In her new enthusiasm for her field, she had come to assume that the psychological way of seeing life transcended all other ways, and that naturally Sheila, like everybody else, would share her enthusiasm. Pam found it hard to believe that Sheila could criticize her unremitting concentration on problems of human interaction and insist that she was dangerously ignoring the political, social, or cultural context. However, she knew Sheila was sincere, and she was relieved that her criticisms didn't mean total rejection, only a postponement of intimacy for a while.

Sometimes when one of an old pair of friends has changed and the friendship no longer seems tenable, he or she may still attempt to salvage it through candid discussion. If this doesn't work, the friend being rejected has no real alternative but to accept the situation as gracefully as possible. This, at least, allows for a possible revival of the friendship someday. Continued bitter protests will only ensure that the waning friendship will turn into an actual enmity, which precludes a later resumption of the friendship.

In handling our resources of space, time, and emotional capacity for relationships, we face many moments of decision when a potential friend asks, in effect, whether we want to become friends. We must beware of the almost imperceptible concessions to our own busy schedules and other commitments which at such critical moments can lead us to cut ourselves off from the newness, the unpredictability, and the spontaneity that give life to friendships.

11.

Crossing the Barriers

Friendships are easy and safe when they develop between two people who are alike. On the other hand, there is a curious factor in friendships that parallels what anthropologists studying marriage call exogamy—the tendency, or sometimes the requirement, to marry outside your own tribe. While it is true that most people choose most of their friends or lovers from within their own cultural group, a certain proportion choose from outside their group. This tends to be most prevalent in situations such as the armed services or college dormitory life, when people are under stress or removed from family and class restrictions on potential friendship. In ordinary life situations we also notice unusual assortments of friends which, in various ways, break through the barriers of ethnic group, class, age, or family background. Sometimes the exogamy factor is at work; for instance, there are WASP's who have mainly Jewish friends and Catholics or ex-Catholics who have mainly Protestant friends. Sometimes other factors are involved; upwardly mobile people, for example, tend to leave behind their ethnic origins and often have few friends from their original group.

There is an undeniable attractiveness, as the saying "opposites attract" tells us, about people who are different or whom you take to be different. It can be fascinating to be with a friend you feel you'll never entirely understand;

you know there will always be some irreducible mystery there. Yet, fundamentally different attitudes or behaviors can also be deeply frustrating and alienating. If you confine yourself to people from your own "tribe," you can avoid much confusion or unexpectedly difficult situations; you know where you are, but that sometimes can be dull. So we suggest it's worth going to considerable lengths to cultivate and maintain friendships with people who are different.

Alison habitually explored friendship possibilities across any barriers she happened to encounter. When she was 32, she struck up a friendship with Laszlo, a 65-year-old gardener and carpenter. Alison was a zoological illustrator; Laszlo, who had come to Boston from his native Hungary after World War II, was a fanatic plant lover; and they met among the bromeliads. Alison remembers that what impressed her was that Laszlo had more enthusiasm, energy, and interest in the world than most people her own age. He was also courtly and cultured, whereas most of Alison's younger friends tended to be rather casual.

Alison and Laszlo discovered they shared another important interest: symphonic music. While some of Laszlo's friends ranged up to and beyond his own age, others were much younger; age was not a matter that Laszlo had ever paid any attention to. He himself lived on very little money, from freelance work. His unorthodox lifestyle and European perspective were constantly refreshing to Alison, who had spent much of her life trying to escape her Midwestern WASP insurance-executive family upbringing.

Alison and Laszlo had thus far transcended their age disparity with ease; what gave them trouble was sorting out the friendship and sexual aspects of their relationship.

At this time, Alison had three concurrent lovers. She had found, after being married and living with several other men, that she was unlikely to find everything she wanted and needed through a relationship with only one man. She was not interested in remarriage or a family. When she became friends with Laszlo, she was seeing—each about once a week—her former live-in lover, a painter; an intellectual with whom she went disco dancing; and a lobster fisherman who owned a small house on the coast. She also had numerous friends of various ages.

Laszlo had been married, and his children had grown up and left home. He had sexual relationships from time to time, but at the moment he had no steady partner. He was more and more taken with Alison's free spirit and vitality and her ability to dress stylishly on a thrift-shop budget. They began making botanical field trips on the weekends. They would hike together along beaches, through cranberry bogs, or on remote country roads. After one of these outings, Laszlo took her to his tiny cottage outside the city and cooked a magnificent goulash, with plenty of good wine to go with it. Carried away with their general good feelings from the day, they fell into bed and made love.

Alison did not attach much importance to this event, but Laszlo did. In short, he fell in love and began to seek more of Alison's time. Alison explained to him that as much as she prized their friendship, she felt quite committed to her other three lovers; Laszlo could not expect sex to be a major aspect of their relationship, though they could occasionally make love. Even so, Laszlo began to fantasize about their future together. To a person of his generation and character, the kind of warm, joyous relationship he had with Alison was something that would inevitably lead to deeper and deeper commitment.

Alison might have averted some of the ensuing complications if she had foreseen that the sexual contact to which she gave minor importance would thus come to have so much importance for Laszlo. Alison had made a practice of remaining open to the needs and desires of the person she was with but always preserving her own independence. She had had sexual friendships with many men of her age without difficulty, so she saw no problem in following her impulses with Laszlo.

Soon, however, Laszlo's impassioned demands began to wear upon her, though she loved Laszlo, in her way, and was flattered by his attentions. Finally, she told him firmly that he must choose between being a nonsexual—or virtually nonsexual—friend or an abandoned ex-lover; she also told him she would not see him for several months, to let things cool off.

Laszlo was crushed. Given his experience and wisdom, we might have expected him to have understood more readily how attached Alison was to a way of living that could not accommodate exclusive sexual relationships. But he found this excruciatingly difficult. He recalls that he retreated to his cottage and brooded. He spent some weeks meditating, tending his gardens, and listening to many hours of music on his stereo. He wondered whether his mistake was in hoping for Alison's exclusive favors, or whether she was turning from him because of his age. When he phoned Alison in bad moments, she would patiently explain that she had been willing to give him the occasional status of a fourth lover but could not give him more, and that she was unwilling to give up any of the others. She made it clear that their age difference was not a factor; the trouble was that he had pushed beyond the bounds she set for a sexual friendship.

Laszlo gradually accepted the realities of the situation. He is proud now of having overcome his raw feelings and of having accepted the disappointment of Alison's rejection. He saw that he was in danger of allowing his wounded feelings to end the friendship, but he also knew that he was extremely fond of Alison. Somehow this gave him the resilience he needed. He gradually realized that it was up to him to find a satisfactory emotional and sexual relationship with another woman. Once he had accepted this responsibility, though it took him a long time to carry it through, he was able to see Alison again without putting any pressure on her. She was then willing to resume their botanical expeditions and symphony attendance. She also made it clear to him that she admired and was touched by his ability to salvage their friendship at the cost of his hopes for love.

We find the relationship between Alison and Laszlo heartening because it triumphed in a beautiful and resilient way over the twin obstacles of age and sex. Throughout, Alison prized Laszlo's age because it gave him patience, compassion, and tolerance from which she could learn; and Laszlo prized Alison's age because it gave her a boldness, adventuresomeness, and spontaneity which inspired him. Their friendship, when it was tested, proved too valuable to lose.

Especially in suburban communities, America still tends to be an age-stratified society; people are seldom in contact with others of markedly different ages. However, we have observed in the last few years that the age barrier to friendships has begun to crumble, perhaps partly because our population now contains a much higher proportion of older people. Also, Americans have recently been gaining a greater understanding of the aging process; and because older people are seen as less alien and thus more equal—an essential requirement for friendship—friendship across the generational barrier seems less difficult.

For example, the revelation that older people normally can continue sexual activity into their eighties and nineties has made them seem more vital to younger persons; and the relaxation of forced retirement regulations is enabling people to work beyond age 65. There are many examples of distinguished and energetic scientists, politicians, and artists who remain active through all the cycles of life; they continue to participate fully in their fields and make significant contributions that are widely recognized and appreciated. Their age is immaterial. Such people, with their hopeful emphasis on positive energy, looking forward and not to the past, usually have friends of all ages.

Edward and Beatrice, who are almost 80 years old, have friends of various ages, even into the twenties. As Beatrice remarks: "Most people our age have already died." Young people find them fascinating, partly because they bely the unfortunate stereotype of dull "old folks" living in the past; they lead busy, active lives. Edward is a travel writer, and Beatrice writes cookbooks. Thus, despite their years, they are engaged in meaningful and remunerative work that requires them to stay in touch with the experiences and tastes of other generations. They entertain fairly often and are widely considered to be excellent hosts; people of all ages are delighted to be invited to their home.

We think that the key to their ability to relate across the age barrier is their genuine interest in what they do. As Edward says: "We have never thought of ourselves as outside the mainstream of life." They take it for granted that what they have to say will be of interest to people of any age level. They feel themselves to be producers—of ideas, experiences, and information—and their creative enthusiasm is contagious. Of course, they have certain restrictions on their physical activity and even, to Beatrice's disgust, on their diet, but they rarely focus their own or anybody else's attention on these. Their happy if often tumultuous relationship is another aspect of their life-embracing attitudes, and younger people are often astonished that they find their marriage fresh and exciting after almost sixty years.

For their part, Edward and Beatrice are deeply intrigued by young people. They appreciate their energy, idealism, and ambition; even when their greater experience tells them that their young friends are perhaps being a little foolish, they try to refrain from saying anything discouraging or cynical. They aid young people with projects, help make useful contacts for them, and offer constructive criticism of their work. Their young friends realize that Edward and Beatrice, despite their intellectual vigor, do sometimes need help in meeting day-to-day problems, and can accept such help graciously and without feeling dependent. In such cross-age friendships, as in any friendship, it is essential that both sides accept and respect the other's varying strengths and weaknesses.

One aspect of the art of friendship is to be conscious of the effects of the different stages of life on our friendship patterns. As we move through life, some obstacles to friendship diminish while others arise. Becoming a parent usually signals a major change.

As we noted in the previous chapter, parents tend to have much less free time than nonparents, since a great portion of their energy goes into child care during the first years of their children's lives. Thus, they not only feel less available for their friends, but they are so. During this period, they tend to concentrate their friendships among other parents, who understand their situation, live in roughly the same way, and whose children can play with theirs while the adults socialize. For many, this seems more natural than friendships with childless people. Because child-centered friendships focus on the health and well-being of the children, they often develop considerable intensity. But as children get older or a remarriage occurs or one couple moves or circumstances change (more money can mean more babysitters and thus less interdependence, for example), these child-centered friendships tend to wither.

In friendships between people who become close while they are single, the marriage of one and subsequent birth of a child can become real obstacles to continued friendship. Elizabeth, a single woman in her late twenties, had never had any children and had no intention of ever having any; she was also disinclined to marry. She had a good job, led a busy life, had numerous friends and acquaintances, and earned enough money to take vacations, buy expensive clothes, and have a sporty two-seater car.

One of her best friends was Marie, with whom she had grown up. When Marie first moved to Atlanta, where Elizabeth lived, they renewed their relationship with great enthusiasm. They went out dancing and to the movies; they took trips together; they organized impromptu picnics and excursions; they got drunk and stayed out till three o'clock in the morning. In time, Marie developed a serious relationship with Roger and started living with him. Elizabeth got along well with Roger, so Marie's relationship with him did not interfere with their friendship. Elizabeth and one of her men friends often went out with Marie and Roger, and she and Marie continued to do a lot of things together. When Marie announced that she and Roger were getting married, Elizabeth was pleased for both of them.

A few months after the wedding, Marie became pregnant. Elizabeth says that she found herself less than overjoyed at this development, and she had twinges of anxiety that it foreshadowed serious changes in the relationship. When Marie sometimes talked to her about prenatal examinations and other experiences Elizabeth could not share, she felt excluded; and when Marie began buying baby clothes, repainted what was to be the baby's room, and became a bit reluctant—due to her bulging belly—to run about at Elizabeth's usual hectic pace, Elizabeth realized she felt downright resentful. She was ashamed of this, however, and did not speak of it to Marie; once the baby was born, she thought, things would return to normal and the fun would resume. And Marie, caught up in the joyous process of pregnancy, did not notice Elizabeth's discomfort; she blithely assumed Elizabeth was as devoted to her pregnancy as she was. This lapse in communication was not to be remedied for a long time.

When Erica was born, Elizabeth thought she was a dear little thing. Once Marie and Erica returned home from the hospital, however, the problems Elizabeth had dreaded began to arise. Elizabeth would telephone to talk with Marie, who wouldn't be able to talk—either the baby was sick, or Marie was in the middle of feeding her, or some pressing baby- or house-oriented task had to be accomplished. Sometimes Elizabeth and Marie would make plans to go somewhere together; but when Elizabeth arrived, she'd find that the baby had disrupted the plans in some way, and Marie would propose that they just sit around the house and drink some wine—which Elizabeth regarded as a distinctly second-rate way of spending an evening, especially when it meant abandoning something she had had her heart set on doing.

Matters were made more difficult for Elizabeth when it turned out that Roger and Marie had agreed that since Roger was now working harder as the sole supporter of the family, they would adopt the traditional pattern, and

Marie would attend to virtually all of the child-care as well as household responsibilities, though previously they had shared the housework pretty equally. Elizabeth, as an independent, equality-minded person, thought that Roger should share equally either in the housework or the child care, not only because that would be fair but because it seemed important to her that Erica should see her father as a nurturing and present person, too.

Elizabeth suggested to Marie that a portion of the housework could be taken over by a hired person so that each parent expended an equal amount of time and energy on family matters. Marie, however, thinking of the precarious state of the family budget and perhaps also secretly relishing her control over Erica's upbringing, refused to consider this possibility. Since Marie had been earning more money than Roger, Elizabeth then counterproposed that *he* stay home and take care of Erica and the house and Marie return to work. Marie vehemently rejected this idea, arguing that in the first year, especially, when a baby is nursing, it needs its mother's full attention; besides, she admitted, she didn't think Roger would be willing to become a "house-husband" and cope with diapers and mashed bananas, as she was willing to do.

This argument shook both women. Marie felt there might be some justice in Elizabeth's attacks on Roger and their new arrangement, but she was not willing to contemplate changing it at this point. Elizabeth was disturbed because although Marie and Roger seemed perfectly happy in their new life, she was sure that Marie was repressing some anger at the situation. Elizabeth was also upset because Marie and Roger, as a couple, had not worked the matter through in the way Elizabeth believed a modern, liberated couple should. Elizabeth's liking and respect for Roger eroded; and when he was not around, she found herself wondering if she could refrain from saying critical things about him. And it became harder for her to spend time alone with Marie and the baby as well.

Part of Elizabeth knew that the joys and pleasures Marie received from caring for Erica must be extremely intense and rewarding, and perhaps more than out-weighed the imbalance Elizabeth saw in the situation. But since she had never had a child herself, she could not understand the power of the biological bond, especially between a nursing mother and her baby, but also between Roger and the baby. When Roger or Marie attempted to explain to her the pleasure they were now taking in their rather home-centered lives, Elizabeth could respond only with impatience.

Elizabeth also noticed with a twinge of jealousy that Roger and Marie had begun to spend a good deal of time with other married couples who had young children. It was this which forced her to accept the fact that Roger and Marie had really entered a new phase and to decide whether she was willing to make a real effort to put her friendship with Marie on a new footing. In thinking the situation over, Elizabeth says that she found it useful to discuss it with some of her single friends. Practically all of them had experienced similar difficulties in relationships with people who had begun to have children. In one way or another, they all advised her to admit to herself that Marie had the right to live her life any way she wished to, even though Elizabeth would do it quite differently; she had to respect Roger and Marie's right to make decisions in their own way, even if she felt they were mistakes.

Once she had faced this, Elizabeth found it easier to talk to Marie about her problems with the new situation; and Marie, sensing Elizabeth's more accepting attitude, was able to be more candid about the ambiguities in her own feelings. They both realized that their friendship meant a great deal to them and that they would have to take special steps to ensure that it remained healthy. Marie decided to set aside time to spend alone with Elizabeth in ways that were rewarding to both of them; and Elizabeth, for her part, recognized that her resentment of Erica's presence had blinded her to the very real satisfactions that a relationship with a child can offer. She found she could attend picnics and other family events, at which the baby's presence happily reminded her of her own childhood, without feeling that she was missing more exciting adult-oriented activities. When she went to dinner with the family and Erica got bothersome, she never altogether overcame her resentment of what she still saw as interference, but she did learn to accept these feelings as part of a friendship which, after all, offered many more rewards than frustrations.

Parents often feel that their friends who have no children do not have a basis for their opinions about child-rearing practices. Childless people, on the other hand, often feel that parents get so caught up in a child-centered world that they lose their adult perspective and short-change their own lives. And sometimes people who otherwise wish to be friends find issues concerning child-rearing practices to be insuperable barriers to continued friendship.

Harry had been friends with Mark and Elaine for some years. Harry and Mark were friends partly because of a shared interest in sailing, though this was difficult for them to maintain because neither of them ever had much extra money. Elaine and Harry liked each other as well. She had an antique press in the basement on which she printed elegant cards, posters, and prints; and he appreciated the skill and artistry of her work. The three friends hung around the boat harbor together on weekends, went sailing on the little boat they jointly owned, and frequently ate dinner together.

After some years, Mark and Elaine got married and soon had two children. All went well for a time. Harry and Mark still managed to go sailing, though Elaine wouldn't take the children out on the boat. When the children were about 5 and 6 years old, however, Harry found himself increasingly uncomfortable around them. The son, who was older, would torment his sister maliciously, and the parents would discipline him ineffectually; indeed, Harry suspected that in some way, Mark and Elaine condoned the child's behavior. The daughter was developing a pattern of tattletelling, which she knew would lead to at least momentary revenge on her tormentor.

Mark and Elaine were extremely gentle souls who never openly expressed aggression themselves. Their attitude toward the children's aggression seemed to Harry to be ambivalent. On the one hand, they could hardly believe that their darling son could actually be doing the mean things he forced them to witness. On the other, they felt such behavior needed punishment—though they were reluctant to punish anybody, since they felt that punishment was itself a form of aggression. The result was that they vascillated: either they gritted their teeth and endured the children's behavior, or they fell prey to bouts of lost temper, excessive punishment, and embarrassment in front of Harry and other friends. Harry also suspected that the kids picked times to misbehave when other people were around, sensing their parents' unease.

Harry finally concluded that he couldn't go on seeing his friends when their children were present. He still went sailing with Mark but that became less and less frequent and gradually the friendship waned. If Harry had been able to bring the matter out into the open, he might have helped Mark and Elaine see the problem from another perspective; this could have enabled them to deal with it, which in turn could have deepened the friendship. But perhaps the question was, as he sensed, so touchy and so deep-rooted that nobody but the couple themselves could really cope with it. In any case, it was not until the children were in school and were forced to change their neurotic patterns because of their contact with other children that their behavior improved to the point at which Harry again felt comfortable in the house. One sign of the children's effect on the adult relationship was that Harry never accepted an invitation to go sailing with the whole family.

Some people do not retreat from confronting difficult situations the way Harry did. Madeleine knew a couple whose children (then ages 5 and 8) constantly interrupted adult conversations, yet the parents made no attempt to control them. This puzzled Madeleine. She recalls wondering why the parents, who were both bright and observant, didn't send the children to their room to play. She finally brought the matter up hesitantly and discovered that both parents, without being conscious of it, felt on the basis of their own childhood experiences that the presence of a parent was essential at all times to mitigate the bickering and unpleasantness of sibling rivalry and conflict.

Madeleine and her friends talked the situation over, and Madeleine cautiously pointed out that many children spend large amounts of time together without much trouble, and indeed often enjoy it. The parents revealed their own resentment of having constantly to be "on duty" and agreed to allow the children to play together unsupervised. This arrangement worked out rather well. Not only were the parents able to enjoy each other and their company far more than before, but they were grateful to Madeleine for trusting their friendship enough to bring the problem out into the open.

The issues that the presence or behavior of children can raise may be painful on both sides. Unsolicited advice about parenting is usually taken as implied criticism and is thus often resented; but here the risk proved worth taking, partly because of Madeleine's skill in handling the situation. Since people's feelings about child rearing are so intense, successful discussions about it can lead to a greater degree of intimacy. Madeleine reflects that in a society made up of extended families where child rearing was a responsibility more widely borne, people would receive more feedback about their handling of children—their own children and others'—and thus take it more as a matter of course. In such a society, too, childless persons would have more routine contact with children, and the differences in roles between parents and nonparents who were friends would be less divisive.

Given that the United States is supposedly a society on the road to racial integration, we have been surprised at how rarely durable friendships develop across racial lines. Models of such friendships are now sometimes offered in fiction, film, or on television, but in real life a common interest—most often professional—may lead to frequent association but seldom does this result in intimacy or continued personal contact. Very young children mix easily across racial lines in school settings and in racially integrated neighborhoods; class divisions are also unimportant in early childhood. But, sadly enough, by the time children reach fifth or sixth grade, peer pressures usually prevent them from continuing the interracial friendships they formed earlier.

During the political upheavals of the sixties, both in the civil-rights movement and the anti–Vietnam War movement, many interracial friendships sprang up. For people in these movements, brotherhood and sisterhood were the overriding ethical and political imperatives of the day, and they made serious attempts to develop friendships regardless of race. When people saw each other daily and engaged in bitter political struggles together, they often developed strong bonds. Entering a hostile town together on a desegregation campaign and being subjected together to threats, harassment, and the possibility of death, made many differences disappear.

During the late sixties, however, black and white people diverged politically. Black Power as a movement was separatist, except for the West Coast–based Black Panthers, and white political energy was increasingly focused on the draft protests and war resistance. The friendships which grew up in the sixties have now mostly faded, though in certain areas or political subcultures they have been sustained.

Ned, who has been a radical since his student days, feels that there are more interracial friendships today among working-class people than among his mostly middle-class friends, perhaps because working-class people often have more interracial contacts in their job situations. Ned continues to frequently see two black friends he retains from the days of the civil-rights struggle. They work together on political campaigns and invite each other to parties; but, Ned says with regret, they seldom simply spend time together the way they did in the sixties.

Ned emphasizes that political convictions remain for him a basic criterion in determining whether another person might become his friend. During his twenties, it was hard for him to associate at all with people whose views he opposed. Now, though he describes himself as less hard-line and more conscious of the ambiguities of life, he still finds it difficult to befriend anyone whose basic political assumptions are markedly different. As he points out:

"Your politics affect everything you do. Your life choices reflect, whether consciously or unconsciously, your political priorities and values." As a result, Ned finds it hard to contain himself when someone is engaged in work or other activities that seem to him immoral or exploitative; and his outspokenness on this score has, he realizes, created stumbling blocks to friendships that otherwise might have blossomed.

However, Ned feels that his recent friendships are based more on a common sensibility than on a shared, particular political position. He likes people who are intellectual, share his general left-wing politics, and have a critical, skeptical turn of mind yet are reverent about life's potentialities. People, he says, can have different configurations of these qualities and still interest him, but they must have some underlying quality he calls, with a smile, "soul." If that is there, and the basis of the friendship is deep, the friendship may thrive even in the face of fairly serious political disagreements.

Differences in class seem to be almost as insuperable a barrier to friendship as differences in race. Though America, like other industrial societies, has considerable vertical mobility, it is highly stratified except for certain enclaves such as college communities, where class distinctions are muted. Most middle-class persons have friendships only with other middle-class persons, a phenomenon which undoubtedly impoverishes the friendship possibilities of American life.

Beverly is unusual in having several friends outside her own middle-class status and origins. She attributes this to her upbringing: although her father was a doctor, the household was a many-sided one, with relatives around all the time who held much lower social positions. This accustomed her, from childhood on, to being with people who never had any money to spare, lacked formal education, and had working-class attitudes and manners.

Like Ned, Beverly is a dedicated radical; her life as an organizer has brought her into intimate contact with people from working-class origins; and in the process, she has become friends with several people who live outside the middle-class pattern.

Beverly recognizes that class origins and present economic situation affect potential friendships quite differently. Most of Beverly's friends follow a relatively middle-class way of life, while others are quite well off and still others make do resourcefully on very small incomes. One of her best friends, Rosa, who is now an artist, comes from a working-class communist family. Beverly notes that it is easier for her to relate to a person such as Rosa, who has obtained a good education and lives in a relatively class-neutral way, than to somebody who lives entirely in the working-class culture. To Beverly, the crucial factor seems to be whether people feel trapped by their class status or not. Rosa, whose parents taught her the importance of intelligence and political understanding, feels confident that she could live in a higher-income mode if she chose to direct her energies in that direction; consequently, she is comfortable around Beverly and her other middle-class friends.

Another friend, Sarah, whom Beverly met when they lived in adjacent apartments, also comes from a working-class background but lacks Rosa's education. Sarah has been a key-punch operator for seven years and believes she will never be able to rise much above her current position. Unlike Rosa, Sarah feels insecure around people to whom she attributes middle-class characteristics; half-jokingly, she rants to Beverly against "hippies," whom she perceives as "middle-class goof-offs" enjoying a life of laziness, promiscuity, drugs, and flirtations with revolution, secure in the knowledge that they "can go home" to a middle-class lifestyle if they feel like escaping the duress of poverty.

An exceptional cross-class friendship developed between Rick, a functionary in a state office, and Danny, a maintenance worker in a steel mill. Both had a serious weight problem and had enrolled in a weight-reduction clinic. The clinic happened to assign them as "buddies" to monitor each other's progress (or backsliding) during the program and to provide each other with moral support as needed.

The clinic utilized encounter-group techniques to help the members understand the psychological origins of their condition. Rick and Danny, like the others in their group, bared their bodies (for the weekly weigh-in) as well as their souls. Because the men were encouraged to express the anguish, depression, and anger, which their habitual overeating was seen as an attempt to assuage, the therapy sessions often included painful self-revelatory scenes going far beyond the immediate problems of weight. Rick had just gotten divorced; Danny was having a troubling sexual relationship and missed his son, who lived with his mother in a distant city. Such problems, of course, are not basically class-defined, though their expression is class-influenced.

Over a period of time, Rick and Danny began to understand and trust each other. When Danny told Rick about his warehouseman-father's blind rages, which once led him to literally throw an armchair out the window, Rick could empathize, although his own professor-father's blind rages involved gnashing his teeth as he bent the family silver into pretzel-shaped pieces. Danny's mother was a stout, long-suffering martyr; but his relationship with her was not that different from Rick's with *his* mother, who was an insufferably thin former teacher.

The two men proved their mutual steadfastness in keeping to the weight-reduction program, and both were gratified that they steadily continued to lose weight and to feel better. They took to jogging together several times a week and discovered that they had considerably more in common than too many pounds and unhappy family backgrounds. Since they knew so much about each other's intimate problems, they could hardly be intimidated by the fact that they came from different class backgrounds or had different lifestyles. Gradually, they evolved what we call a single-purpose friendship, oriented specifically around one area of concern: their continued emotional welfare and persistence in maintaining their weight loss. They saw each other regularly for jogging or other athletic endeavors; they gave each other advice, quizzed each other skeptically about new developments in their lives, and checked out each other's weight, posture, and bodily alignment.

On several occasions, feeling good about each other, they experimented with expanding their friendship into other areas, thinking it might develop into the kind of "multi-purpose" relationship that people regard as the most satisfying kind of friendship. Once Rick invited Danny to a party at his house; but Danny felt uncomfortable among Rick's fellow bureaucrats and their spouses, so Rick never repeated the invitation. And Danny once took Rick to the miniature auto races he enjoyed so much, but Rick was bored by the endless time comparisons and discussions of engine refinements. They accepted the fact that their friendship had relatively narrow limits and recognized that even so, it was real and important to both of them.

If friends begin to move in incompatible directions in politics, religion, or lifestyle, they may face painful obstacles to continuing their association. Martha and Ray were social workers in San Antonio. During the sixties, they led an easygoing married life in an old house near the river. They discreetly smoked dope, helped in occasional political campaigns, and contributed to civil-rights groups. Their circle of fellow spirits was small but lively, and they became especially friendly with one couple, Joe and Ruth. The four of them had long, rambling discussions at their barbecues, shared the care of the six children they had among them, and went on leisurely boating and fishing expeditions. Joe and Ruth were especially critical of the dominant American corporations, opposed the intensification of the Vietnam War, and disdained a life oriented toward consumption and material goods. They built their own furniture, cooked vegetarian delights with foods from their own garden, and developed an interest in Oriental religions. One summer, they traveled through Asia in a camper, visiting temples and spiritual centers, and attempting to live not as tourists but as members of the local communities.

Upon their return, Joe and Ruth were even more embittered about "the system," but to Martha and Ray's surprise, something about their foreign experience had seemingly led them to give up on humanity—including their own. Joe, who had been an electrician, started an electronics firm, which soon prospered on government contracts. He and Ruth no longer showed interest in attempts to improve society or help others. They even boasted of cheating a Mexican mechanic who had worked on their car. They moved out of the old neighborhood into a flashy suburban house.

Now, though they still felt contempt for the American Way, they no longer voiced criticisms of it and refused to engage in the freewheeling talks they had once enjoyed with Martha and Ray. Though they still invited them to their house occasionally, Martha and Ray felt there wasn't much to talk about. All Joe and Ruth seemed interested in figuring out was how they could use other people in social climbing and feathering their own nest—and Martha and

Ray were obviously of no use to them. Joe also developed the odd habit of wandering off to his den during the evening, claiming that his business worries made him too nervous to talk comfortably.

After pursuing increasingly divergent lifestyles for several years, both sides realized that the friendship was no longer tenable. Joe and Ruth had come to view their old friends as liabilities and embarrassments. Perhaps feeling guilt at their selfishness in coping with their disillusionment, they displaced it as anger against Martha and Ray, accusing them of being hopelessly idealistic and naïve. Their marriage began to crumble, which further increased their resentment of Martha and Ray, who were still quite happy together.

Martha and Ray felt sad and bitter; they missed their earlier close friendship with Joe and Ruth and felt betrayed; and when they realized they had lost their respect for Joe and Ruth, they knew the friendship was over.

We cannot leave the subject of obstacles to friendship without mentioning several technological developments which, we believe, have significant but largely unappreciated consequences for our friendship patterns.

Americans spend on the average about five hours a day watching television—more time than they spend on any other waking activity, except work. We find this statistic distressing because in a more relationship-oriented society those five hours would be devoted to family, friends, exercise, education, or other human-related activities. It is hardly an exaggeration to say that the television set is many Americans' best friend. It gives us our information; it fills up our time; it minds our children; and it relieves us from being active or taking risks that might lead to growth. By "killing" time with TV, we prevent those unpredictable, spontaneous happenings that contribute to friendship. If we are glued to the television set, we certainly don't get the idea of going out for a friendly walk. We don't notice that our companion seems to be worried about something or ask what it is, which could lead to an exchange of feelings and mutual support; we don't cope with other people's feelings; we don't get to have interesting arguments; we don't even discuss what is going on in our lives. In short, television is a massive social analgesic balm. The social and personal costs of our national addiction to television watching are incalculable, but friendship is certainly among the chief casualties.

Another technological device with questionable effects on friendship is the telephone. Many women living in traditional homemaker isolation have found the telephone a precious connection to the outside world. Middle-aged or older women sometimes admit that during their early child-rearing years, when they were expected to stay at home alone with their children, they would literally have gone out of their minds without the opportunity to talk with a friend on the phone for an hour or so every day. On the other hand, some people feel that our reliance on the telephone tends to separate us from each other by replacing direct human contact with contact through the intermediary of a mechanical device. Few Americans are willing to risk living without a phone, but those rare people who have deliberately tried it report that it *does* improve their relations with friends: they spend less time in unimportant chitchat; they experience more pleasure in unplanned visiting; and they live more in the present without that typical American feeling of wondering when the phone will ring.

Another great American technological device, the car, has clearly had serious effects on our friendship patterns as well. By isolating us much of the time as we drive, the car reduces our sociability and, like the telephone and television, accustoms us to the idea that a large portion of our important dealings are with machines, not people. We must grudgingly admit, though, that the car is a great help to teenage social life, since it enables teenagers to escape the limitations of the family circle.

Of course, there are some areas in which our technology seems to have been a considerable aid to the development of friendships. For instance, for many people, feelings of kinship are readily generated through a shared enthusiasm for films and for music. The easy availability of a wealth of music on the radio and in tape or record form has thus meant that people can connect emotionally through the music they love.

12.

Creative Friendship

It is perhaps surprising that so many of us treasure certain friends for their upbeat qualities, their courage and optimism, their pluck in the face of adversity, and their positive contributions to the friendship, while we ourselves make little attempt to reciprocate by developing our own strengths in these areas. As Joel comments sadly, his greatest regret about his past friendships is that he wasted so much of the time he spent with friends focusing on his sorrows, despairs, and problems. Looking back, he realizes that he could just as easily have devoted his time with these friends to positive interaction—sharing moments of pleasure and joy, actively planning for better times to follow the bad, and trying to give something to the friends rather than just taking what they offered or grasping at them for comfort.

Joel, like others who have learned to handle their friendships more skillfully, now sees that it is at least as important for a friend to know how to contribute energy, attention, ideas, support, and care as to be open enough to make his or her needs for these things known. Both these capacities must be present in both friends; otherwise, the giver has the best of it—it really *is* more blessed to give than to receive because the giver is gratified by feelings of strength and generosity as well as by the friend's pleasure and gratitude.

Whatever your skills in friendship, your life can always benefit from examining your friendships systematically and setting out to improve them. Creating more adventurous friendships enriches all aspects of your life—you feel stronger; you feel satisfied at having channeled your emotional capacities into appropriate, rewarding interactions; and you feel renewed by the deeper experiences you and your friends have shared.

Friends who respond to each other sensitively and creatively have come to realize that variety and diversity are key elements in keeping friendships lively and strong. While good friends usually share some common interests, it is a mistake to assume from this that any one friend will share all of your interests or, for that matter, your attitudes and values. (Nor, of course, will any lover fulfill all of your various needs or respond to all of your potentialities.) Thus, you would instinctively phone different friends to confide upsetting news, to ask for a quick ride to the airport, or to tell about a new job. The friend you would most like to go camping with is probably not the one you'd most like to go to a movie with, and the friend you love to attend concerts with is probably not the one you'd ask to accompany you to the dentist for gum surgery. Moreover, you probably have single-purpose friends, with whom you share a limited range of interactions and interests, and multipurpose friends, with whom you might easily do almost anything.

This sense of the specialness of each friendship is an important ingredient in preserving spontaneity and a feeling of growth and change. Each friendship has its own dynamics and should be regarded as a complement rather than a threat to other friendships. The fact that you have a lively, interesting time with one friend doesn't mean you value your other friends less, though you didn't choose to share that particular occasion with them. We must give our friends, and retain for ourselves, the right to choose among the varied possibilities we offer each other. Some friends offer you intellectual stimulation; others offer subtle emotional interchange; and still others are people with whom you share excursions, sports, or other physically active undertakings. With each of your friends you get the chance to be a somewhat different person, developing and strengthening different sides of your character and providing variety and stimulation for your life.

Paying closer attention to the balance of friendships and other commitments in your life can be surprisingly rewarding. Some people need to give a greater emphasis to their friendships in order to avoid putting undue pressure on their mate. Others who have relied upon their sexuality to make human contact need to strengthen their capacity for gratifying nonsexual friendships. And there are a few rare people whose full and satisfying friendship life is carried out at the expense of their possible commitment to a mate or their sexuality; these people need to actually limit the amount of time and energy they devote to their friends. By evaluating your own life balance in these terms, you can more clearly define the directions for your own growth.

People who practice creative friendship have learned that there are a number of common pitfalls which can negate their efforts. There is, for example, the lure of the inaccessible. As Robin says: "You can unconsciously have a kind of Groucho Marx principle at work—Groucho said he wouldn't want to be a member of any club that would accept somebody like him." Robin feels that he has often preferred to concentrate unrequited attention on somebody who realistically was not available as a prospective friend—because of disinterest, geographic distance, class

differences—rather than to cultivate friendships with
other people who have indicated an openness to friendly
contact. "I finally realized this was a loser's strategy,"
Robin says. "I missed out on people who had a great deal
to offer, and those wonderful but inaccessible ones never
noticed I was there."

Another common pitfall is the tendency to classify your
friends into "best friend" and "other good friend" cate-
gories. Having best friends may be an appropriate trait in
adolescence, a highly emotionally charged time of life
when having one friend who understands you and in
whom you can confide totally seems overwhelmingly
important. In later life, however, focusing all your friendship energies on one best friend seems unrealistic and
limiting; in addition, trying to identify one person as your
best friend is usually counterproductive. For one thing, it
may lead you to neglect your other friends. For another,
since friendships are rarely symmetrical, it underlines the
fact that the person you regard as your best friend may
not reciprocate the feeling. Also, designating someone as
your best friend introduces an unwholesome rigidity and
potential for conflict to arise when, as is bound to happen,
your friendship interests change and your best friend
must be "demoted." Usually, most people develop several
differentiated close friendships, which we believe is both
a sound and satisfying approach.

People who strive for greater intimacy in their friendships need to bear in mind that a healthy friendship usually has a balance or cycle of closeness and distance. It's
possible for an important friendship to grow too intense or
overpowering; and if that happens, we must feel free to
retreat from it for a while, giving ourselves space till we
recapture a sense of equilibrium. If we are creative
friends, we are sensitive to these fluctuations in intensity
and recognize the need not to let one friendship over-

shadow the others; and we are also sensitive to the fact that our friend may sometimes feel the need for space whether we are in the mood to provide it or not—and that it is his or her right to feel that way. Our friends never remain fixed quantities; their needs and moods often will not run in perfect synchronization with ours. But these vacillations, if accepted in an understanding way, can actually help "recharge" friendships for another round of development.

Considering our supposedly individualist American ways, it is not easy to understand why so many couples have as friends only other couples, whom they always see in foursomes. Some believe this pattern is an overreaction to traditional social segregation, which separated men's lives and women's lives so strictly that it left the generation of the 1950s with a hunger for "togetherness." We believe that fear of romantic entanglements is a major reason why members of couples tend to have so few single friends. But this is destructive and limiting. Established couples tend to become narrow and stereotyped in their experiences and views of life, forgetting or rejecting the vitality, challenge, and variety which characterize the relationships of independent single persons. We regard it as a danger signal of possible social and personal stagnation if a couple has allowed all friendships with single people to lapse.

A friendship normally entails many kinds of mutual exchange: emotional support, favors and services, gifts. People vary considerably in the "comfort level" of such exchanges. There are deep friendships where nothing material ever changes hands; there are others where a constant stream of small tokens of affection goes back and forth. Trouble arises only when the level and equality of the exchange are threatened by some disparity. Thus, it is difficult for two people to be friends if one is very

thoughtful and caring about gifts while the other is uneasy about them or has difficulty finding anything appropriate to give. And there are people who become uncomfortable if they are given anything at all. Such reluctance
to receive may indicate irrational fears of dependency and
obligation; at any rate, it may constitute an obstacle to
friendship.

Making yourself useful to friends is another kind of exchange, and it can reinforce friendship bonds if it is done
in an unobtrusive way. Helping a friend fix his or her
washing machine is not only concretely useful but a
pleasant way to spend time together around a common
task. As Andy points out: "It's easier for me to relate to
other men and enjoy their company if there is some
project we can play with." The pitfall here is that if one
friend's competence or willingness to help greatly exceeds
the other's, the relationship may degenerate into an unduly dependent one.

As we've said many times, shared interests are a major
foundation of friendships, and the cultivating of our interests is a basic step toward finding new friends. Common interests, however, seem to provide only the soil in
which a friendship may grow; they don't necessarily constitute a sufficient cause for it to flourish. Thus, rather to
our surprise, we discovered that certain kinds of shared
interests do not seem to be nearly as productive of real
friendships as we would have expected. Individual sports
like tennis and running, for example, seldom lead to general, close relationships. Sports friends do, of course,
greatly enjoy playing together and the activity may be
very important to them. The intensity of striving with all
your will and strength against the other player is a kind of
"crisis" in itself; making yourself vulnerable to being de-
feated is a kind of opening-up. These factors do produce
some bonding but evidently of a very limited kind. As

Penny, the runner mentioned in an earlier chapter, points out: "It's hard to be friends with someone you're trying to beat." She spends many hours enjoying potluck suppers and other after-run socializing with fellow runners, but they are never invited to drop over to each other's houses or see each other except in connection with running.

Team sports do seem to generate "locker-room friendships" that extend into outside life areas. Tony, a former basketball player, tells us that this often occurs as a result of the intensely cooperative nature of team effort as well as the camaraderie of being on the road together. He had been close friends for several years with a fellow player with whom he spent time after practice and with whom he shared an interest in high-performance cars. Team players may evolve friendships more easily than individual competitors, who face, in a particularly obvious way, the pitfall posed to friendship by inequality. The consistently weaker player owes a debt to the better player, as it is less challenging and helpful to that person's game to play with a less accomplished player. This principle also applies, of course, to nonsports-oriented relationships, where people aspire to be friends with others who they feel have higher status, more interesting lives, and better contacts.

Creative friendship requires minimizing the negative effects of the factors described above, but even more important it requires maintaining what we call a learning posture. Human beings are intensely social animals. We learn most of what we do (as opposed to what we think) from direct imitation of our parents, siblings, and other early childhood associates. We imitate gestures, sounds, speech patterns, and, most of all, attitudes—some of which we are consciously aware of but many of which remain below the threshold of awareness. A little later we begin to imitate teachers, youthful "heroes" and "heroines," and our peers.

As we become adults, we constantly compare ourselves with others, seeking to imitate their good qualities and examining ourselves to make sure we don't share those that displease or embarrass us. This process can be consciously put to use: if you want to change your behavior, you can deliberately choose a friend on whom you can model yourself. When you see the friend meet a difficult situation skillfully, you observe that skill intently and try to distill its essence so you can incorporate it into your repertoire of behaviors; or after you've faced a difficult situation, you may spend a good deal of time reflecting on how the friend might have handled it. This process is not only practical, since we all have much we can learn from each other, but it weaves us into an overall social fabric of relatively consistent coping behavior.

A surprising number of people feel that they did not learn how to be friends from observing their parents, who either had few friends or carried out their friendship activities away from their children's observation. Some of these people told us of their good fortune of establishing a relationship with someone who had a real gift for friendship, someone who taught them by example what their parents had not.

While there are people who are almost totally self-defined—many of them are found among artists—most of us need to see ourselves through the eyes of others to know who we really are. Some of what friends tell us we discount, of course, but generally we seek as friends people whose feedback feels comfortable—but not *too* comfortable—and on the whole just and fair.

Thus, one of the most valuable things friends give each other is attention. Most of us, in an interpersonal interaction, continually voice our own reactions, suggestions, and evaluations. We want the other person to hear what we have to say, and we're willing to listen to what they have to say because that's the price of being heard. This is not the only way to listen to another person. Another alternative is to withhold your own reactions and to assume the role of a benevolent detective who's intent on reading the clues the friend is revealing, without expressing conclusions, making interpretations, or offering advice or solutions. Some types of encounter groups have had notable success in training people in this kind of patient and observant behavior, partly by the simple device of forbidding them to do anything except question the other person.

This kind of behavior enables you to explore areas of the other person which, if you were busily engaged in telling your own side of the story, you would never notice. It also encourages the friend to reveal himself or herself without being hindered by interjections or asides from you. It requires restraint and self-confidence on your part to give this kind of generous attention. It is not only its own reward once you learn how fascinating it is to practice it, but it also generates a new kind of strength in you, the listener, since it is an ability that elicits such remarkable results.

In this way, you can pay attention not only to your friend but also to the process of your friendship—the ever-flowing emotional interchange, constantly shifting and evolving, that happens between two people. This kind of emotional process fascinates lovers, and they usually spend a good deal of their time talking about their feelings, their relationship, its future, its problems. Many friends, on the other hand, never talk about their friendship at all. Indeed, many friends sense a kind of taboo on any direct discussion of their friendship, perhaps fearing that it would destroy the magical connection between them, just as people sometimes fear that understanding a work of art would destroy their enjoyment of it. Because they feel that open discussions make something less "natural," they worry that talking about their friendship might make it self-conscious and awkward.

This is a concern that we respect, and certainly no one should feel that a friendship is less than it might be if it does not involve any discussion about it. However, we have found that when friends do talk about their relationship, it usually strengthens it, often to the surprise of both friends. They seize the opportunity to clarify misunderstandings, share perspectives on earlier periods and what happened during them, and most important of all, acknowledge openly—and sometimes tearfully—just how much the friendship means to them. We all need to know that we are valued by others, and the explicit statement by a friend that you are one of the really important people in his or her life is a wonderful boost to your self-esteem. It makes you feel more fully human; it makes you feel that life is more worthwhile; it simply and inexplicably warms your heart.

Creative friends are alert to the potential for friendships to reinforce each other. When a friendship network exists, it provides an easy closeness, variety, and resilience. Because your friend Teresa is also a friend of your friend Sloan and his friend Jay, the four of you seem somehow more "familiar," more family-like; you are better known quantities, part of a comfortably mutual social universe.

There is also a certain transferability to friendship. Somehow, when we are introduced to someone who is a good friend of a friend, we extend to that person an openness we would not extend to just anybody we met. A friend "vouches for" another friend, making the new relationship safer and more secure. There is an almost literal transfer of feeling; if you can sense the intimacy of your friend with the other person, you are prepared for the possibility of extending intimacy to that person yourself.

Such infectious friendships may have sexual ramifications. Often people become friends with a friend's lover, for example, and these friendships may outlive the romance that started them. Or an infectious friendship may result in a sexual attraction to the spouse or lover of a friend. The attraction in such cases may stem from some unconscious jealousy or competitiveness—the urge to take for yourself something that is precious to your friend. It is easy to see in a friend's lover the same attractive qualities that the friend loves, and to be touched and tempted by them. In some cases, also, such attractions may be partly an expression of sexual feelings toward the friend, which you forbid yourself to acknowledge. We have found that such subterranean currents of desire flow through most friendships and are sometimes acknowledged jokingly as a way of defusing them. If acted upon, they usually have disastrous consequences.

On the other hand, the fact that people are your friends doesn't guarantee that they will get along with each other. We respond to different aspects of others' personalities; and if two friends have been attracted to markedly different aspects of your personality, they may easily dislike each other—which will hurt and puzzle you if you assume that you will all have wonderful times together. It also happens that two of your friends may be too similar. Muriel, a rather timid woman, has two energetic, assertive women friends. When she introduced them, "They just couldn't agree on anything. They had different approaches to everything, and both of them thought the other was opinionated and inflexible. Worst of all, neither of them could see how I could be friends with the other."

Anyone wishing to practice creative friendship needs to assess the potentials for friendship offered by various living arrangements. Tastes and needs in this area vary widely. Some people prefer to live alone because they know this will stimulate them to put energy into organizing an active friendship life, whereas were they to live with other people, they would make less of an effort to do so. It is more common, however, for people to feel that living alone doesn't provide as much easy contact with a sizable number of people—including potential friends—as does living in a group situation. Many young people, accustomed to living with others in college dormitories, co-ops, or apartments, incorporate this lifestyle into adult life. Beyond its many economic advantages, group living introduces new friendship possibilities. You may straggle home from the office with barely enough energy to warm up a TV dinner and find your roommates preparing a pot-luck supper that will bring ten new people into your life. You help in communal projects that get you out of the doldrums and present you with new experiences. You have the chance to meet new people whom you wouldn't run into in your own circle of acquaintances without going through the party pickup routine. Some roommates develop into close friends; others lead you to people with whom you become close friends. In any event, occupancy of a house or apartment by a group of people, rather than a nuclear family, is a living pattern that more and more people are choosing. It may even turn out that the nuclear family will have been only a transitory phase in the slow evolution of family types; after all, during most of human history we have lived in complex tribal kinship groups, multigeneration families, and other extended family forms. In the years to come, we may find ways to integrate our families of choice into our practical living arrangements.

With a sense of nostalgia, Rodney recalls that his college campus had been an ideal environment for the formation of friendships. "There were lots of common neutral territories—lounges, libraries, cafeterias, and outdoor areas—where people just ran into each other a lot. Even secluded places were safe—you shared the turf." Also, students spend extensive amounts of leisure time in close proximity, which gives them maximum opportunities to interact on a variety of levels and around a variety of interests.

Some architects and planners are attempting to build new structures which permit and encourage such interactions rather than the anonymity and impersonality endemic to so many high-rise apartment complexes. But on the whole, the trend in American architecture is still toward isolation and "security-consciousness."

In the suburbs and in residential neighborhoods of large cities, however, a considerable amount of neighborly spirit still prevails. Neighbors look out for each others' children and property, transmit essential news, borrow food or gardening equipment from each other, and generally do each other small favors or lend a hand when needed. And in some cities, especially where middle-class people are moving back into neighborhoods that had formerly been slums, conscious attempts are being made to recapture this neighborhood vitality. Block associations bring people together on the basis of shared concern over neighborhood problems. Community gardens provide a wholesome outdoor activity that gives a focus for common effort and also provides good, inexpensive food. Solar-energy projects and rehabilitation efforts are sometimes undertaken on a shared basis. All these activities tend to bond neighbors together, decrease anonymity, and foster friendships.

There is something easygoing about neighborhood friendships. Because we often run into neighbors without having to plan to get together, there's a certain built-in spontaneity about relationships with them. We sometimes even spend time with neighbors when we feel too rushed to make dates with our friends; we somehow feel that the time spent with neighbors doesn't "count," so we don't feel guilty about "wasting" it. And because we see neighbors in a variety of roles—fixing the stopped-up sewer line, clipping the bushes, clearing out the garbage, disciplining their children—we get to know them well without making any particular effort to do so. We notice intimate details about how they live: how they behave under challenge to their territory (their lawns or parking spots in front of their houses), how they feel about animals, how open they are to sharing.

It's worth making a serious effort, when you move, to relocate in a neighborhood where some of your friends live—or try to persuade your friends to move into your neighborhood—because that makes seeing them on a casual basis enormously easier. If somebody lives only a block or so away, even though you both live busy lives, you can drop by for a quick drink or cup of coffee, or spontaneously propose going out for a movie, without hassling about the planning and scheduling needed with busy friends who live farther away.

Relationships with neighbors can blossom into solid friendships—and into love affairs and marriages as well. Because there's something realistic and commonsensical about dealings with neighbors which can carry over reliably into long-term relationships, it's wise not to dismiss neighborhood friendships as unimportant. But to explore the creative potential of neighborhood friendships you should probably start with practical objectives. On one Chicago street comprising comfortable single-family houses, a group of three families have become close, reliable friends over a period of ten years. Their children were a very important consideration in the growth of their neighborhood feeling, since they were all concerned with the children's safety and well-being. Perhaps the greatest force in consolidating this friendship constellation was a teacher strike which closed the local schools for an extended period. When the parents first realized that the strike might go on for months, they took the lead in organizing a neighborhood school for the block. The children, bored by having little to do, joined in enthusiastically. The parents who had skills or knowledge that could be put to use organized themselves into a teaching staff. Each week a different house became the schoolhouse, and every Sunday evening the parents gathered to plan the coming week's work. There was a convivial side to the project, as there often is in emergencies; after the meetings, the group would have some wine, sing songs, and generally celebrate their solidarity and determination in putting their values into practice. These contacts, plus the sharing of the tension of waiting for the schools to reopen and confronting the difficulties of running an alternate school, brought the original three couples closer together and closer to their other neighbors as well.

Given the hazards of contemporary urban life, neighbor-friends provide each other with a special sense of security and comfort, which many people feel is an objective worth considerable trouble. Hilda described a wave of burglaries that had alarmed her neighborhood. This caused her neighbor-friends to hold meetings and band together to set up neighborhood patrols in contact with the police. Evidently, news of this spread through the criminal grapevine, because the problem ceased. Hilda reports that after this period, she and her neighbors felt noticeably closer and proud that they had successfully coped with a difficult threat. She had formerly lived in a high-rise apartment, but when trouble—a series of muggings—arose there, people had felt there was nothing they could do except stay inside and watch their step when they went out.

Hilda regards the geographical layout of the houses on her street as an important factor in her relationships with neighbors. The houses all have front porches, which serve as welcoming spots that are both part of the houses and part of the street life. From their windows, the neighbors can see the houses on the other side of the street and thus can see who is around in a way that's difficult with secluded suburban houses. Since Hilda's neighborhood is part of a city, it also has nearby points of common congregation—an ice cream parlor several blocks away, a supermarket a little farther out—to which people can walk together. Traffic is light on the street, so even small children are allowed to play in their front yards without supervision.

One particular appeal of neighborhood friendships is that they help us reconstitute a sense of living in a meaningful society. Many of us spend our days at jobs that are merely sources of income, and our contacts with salespeople and others during the day may also be depersonalized. In our neighborhoods, therefore, where we see each other caring for our children, growing food, repairing our dwellings, and gossiping and socializing together, we can recapture the sense of a social process in which production and consumption are carried out by whole persons we can relate to and not by mechanical functionaries.

Despite the fact that the average American family

moves every three years, neighborhoods are still a source of stability in many lives. And some Americans are realizing that when they need a bigger house, it makes more sense to add a room or two than to uproot themselves and their children from their neighborhood. Isabel, who has had strong neighborhood friendships for more than a decade, says that she and her husband recently considered moving to a smaller house more conveniently located for their jobs, now that their children are grown. But they decided against it. "We just couldn't bear to leave our neighborhood," she says.

Isabel's rosy view of neighborhood friendships is not shared by Deirdre and Clint. They live in a large city partly because they like the city's anonymity and freedom of movement. "Never try to be friends with a neighbor," they say flatly. "You know who they are, you say hello, and that's it. They'll respect you—won't park in your driveway because they don't know if you'll have them towed away." To them, neighborly borrowing is unwise; they had once lent a ladder, only to find their neighbor, after a few months, claiming it as hers. They feel that if you become too close to your neighbors, you give up your freedom and you get involved in neighborhood squabbles about children, property lines, noise, shrubbery. Deirdre and Clint are willing to keep an eye on their neighbors' houses in return for the same, but they prefer to find their friends elsewhere.

On the other hand, some neighbor-friends positively enjoy the subtle hazards of neighborly borrowing. As Anthony puts it: "It can all get quite complicated, but that adds a kind of excitement to the relationship." He does point out that too great an imbalance, where one party is always the borrower, can lead to resentment; and there is, as with anything that can be damaged, the question of trust. He also feels that asking to borrow something means revealing yourself as in some sense improvident and in need. This need must be acknowledged in an easy way on both sides; you must feel that the friend will not take advantage because of the loan, and the friend must feel secure that you will fulfill your part of the bargain.

Privacy can be an issue with any of your friends, but it is particularly tricky for friends who live nearby. The Chicago neighborhood friends mentioned earlier are constantly in and out of each others' houses, but they also respect each others' needs for privacy. As one of them says, if he drops by with a drink in his hand, he knows that he should back off if he sees that a family argument is in progress; on the other hand, as he says: "If I hear ping-pong balls, I know I can expect a welcome."

People who encourage neighbors or friends to drop by without notice usually develop ways of achieving privacy when they really want it. Yvonne and Colin greatly enjoy impromptu cocktail hours and having people count on them for a place to stay when they are in town. While this open-house policy suits them most of the time, they did devise an ingenious way of limiting it when necessary: they set out a little red flag beside their front door, which means, as Yvonne puts it, "that it's shotgun night and anybody who shows up takes the consequences!"

Though neighborhood friendships are often focused on security and stability, a creative friendship life must also provide a sense of adventurousness and flexibility. If you're good at dealing with changes in other aspects of your life, you'll probably handle well the inevitable changes in your friendships. It's important to recognize that a commitment to friendship means a commitment to taking chances. You may pursue a new friend who doesn't respond to your overtures; your attempts to deepen a friendship may end up by jeopardizing it. But we need to remember in such cases that rejection is a disappointment but not a disaster. We'll never like it, but we need not fear it. We can, of course, accept rejection with considerably more equanimity if we have developed a firm confidence in our own essential worth: if we don't reject ourselves, we won't be thrown off balance on those occasions when others reject us.

Creative friendship also requires going beyond your usual limits, pushing yourself a little. Look back over the past year and determine whether you have cultivated any friendships that at first seemed unlikely. If you stuck to people who seemed tried and true and safe, you are probably missing opportunities for growth and stimulation.

One way of expanding your friendship potentialities is to systematically emphasize and nurture sides of your own personality which resonate with models you find in new friends. A person conscious of a desire to live a less dull and routine life may seek friends who are freer and more unconventional. A person who feels that his or her life is too chaotic or unproductive may seek friends who schedule their time effectively, make and carry out plans, and spend their money wisely.

Take stock of your life and identify areas you have neglected or left underdeveloped. If you seldom take chances, you might consider exploring friendships with people who live more adventurously. Some are mental adventurers, who would be willing to read together books you'd never have gotten around to on your own or talk about personal concerns you have never dared discuss. Others are physical adventurers, and though they might not be able to talk you into hang-gliding or sky-diving, you might be willing to go snorkeling or cross-country skiing with them. Try to set aside an occasional weekend day to do something, by yourself or with a friend, that you've never done before. If there are places you've always wanted to visit, but you've never quite managed to follow through on your dreams, keep an eye out for friends who might join forces with you.

Lenore and Connie agreed that they would take turns, once a month, organizing a surprise expedition for the other. They tried to think of gratifying or stimulating things they would never do for themselves or on their own. Connie arranged a glider flight for the two of them, followed by a picnic in the California wine country. Lenore took Connie to a poker club and staked her to a stack of chips so she wouldn't worry about losing money.

Keep in mind the ritual aspects of friendship, for these can be comforts and pleasures in themselves and can also bring about new levels of contact. Burt particularly prizes the ceremonies of life, and his friendships are all marked by ritualized pleasures. Each evening at the same time, he and two neighbors walk their dogs. They also brew beer together, sharing equipment and supplies (and samples!) and a prescribed schedule of fermenting, bottling, and aging. Burt and his friends celebrate all the traditional holidays and have invented some novel ones for themselves: Gallstone Day commemorates the day Burt survived his operation, and Snowfight Day is the day all the families turn out for a good snowball fight . . . if they haven't already had one.

Places can be important aids in creating friendship rituals for yourself. Consider adopting a favorite bar or café where you can feel at home and meet special friends for a regular drink or coffee. If you've found a resort you really like, you could return for next year's vacation with a friend or friends, and make it into a joint tradition. You can invent rituals, big or small, that really suit you and your friends. Vic and Mario developed the habit of playing a little basketball together at a neighborhood playground on Sunday mornings. Although neither of them was terribly athletic, playing just gave them an excuse to get some exercise, which they both needed. They would kid around, exchange stories about their week, and then go for some coffee together. Two couples have a regular "games night" once a month, to which they bring old favorites like Monopoly or Chinese checkers, novelties like the African board game *Ware* or the Hawaiian game *Konane*, or extremely difficult jigsaw puzzles.

Rituals and traditions are also a way of incorporating people of different generations into friendship patterns. Though most godparents no longer have their original religious function of providing spiritual guidance, parents sometimes choose an unofficial godparent from among their closest friends, who is both a mentor for their child and potentially the child's special friend, sharing with him or her the comforting rituals of friendship. Having a grown-up friend helps a child achieve more independence from the parents, whereas having a child friend provides childless adults with a fascinating window into the emotional world of children. Special outings together get such friendships going and give the child experiences the parents may be unable to provide. A child who has experience with adult friends at an early age will find it easier in later years to move into adult relationships within and beyond the family circle. In neighborhoods with a strong friendship tradition, an older person who doesn't work sometimes becomes the "block aunt" or "block uncle" with whom children check in after school or on weekends if their parents are not around or to whom they go for help if an accident occurs.

Some people view with suspicion any regular or ritualized friendship activity. For Katie and Clark, activities that become an obligation soon lose their sense of spontaneity and joy. When they once lived in a small town, they belonged out of desperation to a gourmet club made up of four couples who met once a month at each others' houses on a rotating basis. The aim was to strengthen their friendships and indulge their taste for good food; but in Katie and Clark's view, neither objective was realized. The cooking soon became competitive, with each couple trying to outdo the others; even so, the cooking seldom reached a level that suited Clark, who remarked sourly: "It wasn't bad, if you like *vin rosé* with everything; but all that heartburn sure did put a damper on our friendship campaign." In her kinder way, Katie thinks that any activity which becomes obligatory comes to represent enforced family togetherness at holidays or other occasions. "You can only really enjoy something if you're free to refuse it," she maintains.

Some people seem to have an underlying security about established and potential friendships. They have friends aplenty; and they feel that if they meet someone new with whom they wish to be friends, they can probably bring it off. Such people have confidence in their own friendship skills; they know they are capable of reaching out to someone in a meaningful way, and they know that it is likely that they will receive a favorable response. Thus, they are in the strong position of being able to decide, when they have met someone, whether they wish to move toward friendship. People who are insecure about their capacities for friendship, however, emanate a sense of anxiety and unsureness, which not only makes them uncomfortable but drives away potential friends.

Every person wishing to develop friendships creatively needs to work on the basic, common-sense skills of friendship, which many of us neglect to practice despite their simplicity and straightforwardness. One small but important step is to learn how to deepen conversations with potential friends. We all know people who interest us but with whom we always seem to talk on a light, casual level. Most of us just drift along, hoping that we will somehow break through to greater intimacy. But you can take a more active role in such situations. Pick an opportunity when the two of you have some free, uninterrupted time together alone, and deliberately but gently move the conversation onto a more intimate level by revealing something about yourself—perhaps some secret desire or anxiety, or some special concern or interest you care deeply about. Such a revelation indicates to your friend, without your having to say so in a direct way, that you are open to exchanges of a more trusting nature than you've been enjoying. You extend to the friend an invitation to accept more of you than you've previously revealed and also indicate your willingness to hear similar revelations from the friend. Even if your first attempt at such openness seems trivial, you will find that the next time it will be easier to be more open. This inherently reciprocal process of mutual revelation is, after all, a major part of what we mean when we say we "know" a friend.

Being open to a friend also means being willing to share your opinions. In some relationships, we can go along for years expressing only opinions we're sure our friend will not find strange or offensive; keeping our opinions to ourselves is also a kind of withholding. You can take deliberate steps to minimize this unproductive reticence. Like all human beings, your friend is intensely curious to know what other people, including you, think of him or her. Begin slowly, perhaps by expressing your opinion about how your friend handled some recent situation. (It's wise to start with some area where your opinions are largely positive.) Your friend will be gratified to see that you have taken his or her situation to heart, seriously considered the alternatives it presented, and participated vicariously in the decision. Later on, you can move into areas where you have criticisms of your friend. The objective is to reveal to the friend what you think and how your mind works. Friends are entitled to disagree; in fact, exploring the things you disagree about can be just as intriguing as exploring what you agree on.

It may, of course, sometimes be upsetting. But feelings of anxiety, hesitation, resistance, and awkwardness often indicate that the relationship is moving onto a new level of intimacy. Hang in there, but be sure you are clear about what is going on. When a friendship is growing, you are bound to have some growing pains!

We live in a period when altruism is out of fashion in many circles, and a facile sophistication requires the cynical assumption of base motives behind any seemingly good or kind action. It's almost as if we have been deceived so often by politicians, bosses, teachers, and parents that many people have resolved to think the worst of everyone and never run the risk of deception again. Such a defensive attitude is destructive to friendship and to all human relationships based on mutual concern.

We owe it to ourselves, each other, and our society to combat this thoughtless negativism about the human condition. Friendship cannot exist without trust; it is generous or it is nothing. As we have suggested throughout this book, the vital interchanges of friendship provide us with networks of secure, enlivening, resilient relationships, and mobilize our human potential for warmth, concern, and mutual support, without which we cannot thrive.

About the Authors

Christine Leefeldt is the director of the Humanities Department at the San Francisco Conservatory of Music.

Ernest Callenbach is an editor at the University of California Press in Berkeley and of the magazine *Film Quarterly*. He is the author of *Ecotopia*.

They are married to each other.